INTERNET & WEB DEVELOPMENT
USING HTML, DHTML & JAVASCRIPT

SOMA DASGUPTA

KHANNA BOOK PUBLISHING CO. (P) LTD.
::: *Publisher of Engineering and Computer Books* :::

1694 - 95, Nai Sarak, Delhi - 110006
Phone : 011-23283211   **Fax :** 011-23256658
E-Mail : contact@khannabooks.com
Website : www.khannabooks.com

INTERNET & WEB DEVELOPMENT
SOMA DASGUPTA

ISBN: 81-87522-44-5

Published by :
Khanna Book Publishing Co. (P) Ltd.
1694-95, 1st Floor, Nai Sarak, Delhi-110006 (India)
Phone : 011-23283211 Telefax : 011-23256658
E-mail : contact@khannabooks.com
Website : www.khannabooks.com

Printed in India by:
S.P.S. Printers & Binders, Delhi

Dedicated

to

the students willing to learn

Internet & Web Development

using

HTML, DHTML and JavaScript

Prefatorial Foreword

Seeing the keen Interest of students towards Web Development I have penned this book on Internet and Web Development which includes Internet, HTML, DHTML and Java Script.

I have this fervid belief that the book will guide the students to develop web page step-by-step and improve their skills towards web authoring.

I am thankful to my family, Uday and to Mr. Vivek Khanna my publisher who has given me spontaneous encouragement for gaining the coveted goal same as before.

Every sincerest effort has been energized towards avoiding any omission or commission but if occurred, the same may be excused as a token of sublime generosity.

SOMA DASGUPTA

Contents

INTERNET

1

Concept of Internet

Internet

Networks of computer where you get the worldwide information. Information in any sector – education, business, games and lots more. Actually it's the network of networks.

What are the Internet and World Wide Web?

Not hardware, not software and not even a system? Any company does not own it. So don't confuse, rather you can say it's a place from where you can collect information according to your need and can offer access to people i.e. communication (For ex.- e-mail).

World Wide Web represented by WWW is the part of Internet. Web means the collection of documents, which is created in the hypertext format to make, it accessible through the Internet.

Understanding the Internet

Internet expanded for delivering information in all sectors like Government, Education, Commerce, and Entertainment etc.

For a moment or so think of the place where you live in. What you see and what you do? You buy things from the shops – Now through Internet you can buy things very easily. You are getting a lot of choices to select your product. When you buy things from the shops you are getting the choice available in the shops, but here you can judge the whole worlds market.

Now the question arise how you pay for the goods you buy?

Usually you pay in cash for the items you buy from the shops. Sometimes you may have the risk of carrying cash, which you can't overcome, but while purchasing from the Internet you usually pay by Credit card system, which is more secure and tension free.

Generally these are the commercial sites, which are offering transaction facility over the net.

Communication

Internet offers the mailing facility. Lots of sites offer free mails and chat facility. The use of Electronic mail (e-mail) is common today. Most of the people use e-mail because

1. It's faster than ordinary mail
2. It's secure
3. It's cheap.

Are you connected with Internet?

If you have a computer, doesn't mean you have the Internet connection. What you require is to have your system connected with the network. Then you too can access the net and can avail all its facilities. But it depends what type of connections you are availing. (See the connection details in later section of this book.)

A brief history

In the previous days Internet boom out for the development of Military purpose. The prediction was to improve the defense sector. They developed the network of two to three machines, which communicate at low speeds. Often the network fails due to failure of one machine in the network. So until and unless the machine gets repaired the network stops. So it was very difficult to manage the network. Then the U.S. Department of Defense started performing research and around 1970 the Advance Research Projects Agency part of the Department of Defense developed the ARPAnet.

- The ARPAnet fulfilled many goals.
- The ARPAnet works perfectly even in the failure of one or more computers connected in the network.
- It has the facility of rerouting message if one route fails.
- It works perfectly after connecting with different types of machines having different configurations.
- The ARPAnet had the concepts of server. One machine was connected with network and others are connected with that machine.

But in later days ARPAnet developed with wide research. The outsiders are allowed to use the network and when commercial organizations, educational institutions, government sectors etc. understood the utility of it, they all started entering in the network. To maintain the growth of network a new technology arrived i.e. TCP/IP a protocol that defines about the data transactions. That's the beginning of Internet and it is still growing and it's endless.

Note. Protocol is defined as a set of rules.

Network

We are discussing about the network, let's see how many types of networks are there.

Types of Networks

> LAN – Local Area Network
>
> MAN – Metropolitan Area Network
>
> WAN – Wide Area Network

Importance Of Networking

There is lots of importance of networking, but the most important are as follows

- Files Sharing
- Resource Sharing
- Communication

The users can share the files, they can share the resource for ex.(You will find in many place that their are five computers but a single printer. All the users of the network share the same printer.) And the most important feature of network is communication for ex.(e-mail –electronic mail).

Server and Client

Now it's time to give you the information regarding the Server and the Client. Server stores all the information's and when the Client requests it provides the information. Every machine connected with the net is called as host. Every host has a login name and a password, which allows them to connect the net. The server performs a great role. Suppose a client request a file, which is available in the server it provides the file directly but say if it is not available and the server knows where it is (might be in a different machine, in that case note that the server also became the client), it finds the file for the client, but the client is not knowing how the server is searching the file.

Internet Protocols

Protocols - Now onwards you will find a word protocols. Protocols are a set of rules, which is required for computers to communicate over the net.

And one of the most important protocols, which work side-by-side, is TCP/IP.

TCP/IP

IP the Internet Protocol does the work of searching an address. For ex. You are sending a mail, now IP's work is to search the IP address where the mail will be going. TCP the Transmission Control Protocol does the next part.

It's a packet switching network. It breaks your mail into small packets and it takes the responsibility that your mail reaches at its destination intact. After reaching at the destination it sets your mail in the original sequence. As TCP and IP works together it is referred as TCP/IP.

FTP

FTP the File Transfer Protocol is used to transfer messages between the IP hosts. It is mainly designed for transferring large messages.

HTTP

Everybody is familiar with HTTP the Hypertext Transfer Protocol. HTTP defines how to send and receive the HTML the Hypertext Markup Language files. HTML helps you to format the text files to create the required view for the web browser like headings, paragraphs, images, lists etc. In the later section you will learn the creation of HTML files.

Gopher

Server using Gopher protocol shows the contents in the form of submenus. The client should run the Gopher program to access the files. You can move from one menu to another menu, one file to another or might be from one program to another program just by clicking on the menu items. Still it is not necessary to run the Gopher program but now days it became popular.

Telnet

Just imagine that you are sitting in your machine and logging onto another machine. Using the Telnet protocol you can log onto another machine and can work on it, which makes your machine work like terminal on another.

Do you heard about Intranet?

Now you have an idea about the Internet and the various protocols. So lets start with Intranet – the closed network. Generally the big companies having branches at different places create this network for data sharing and for communication. They find it more secure and cost effective rather than using Internet.

It is an internal Internet, and only the employees of the company can use this network. They create their documents in the form of web pages and place them in the Intranet web servers and all the employees of the company can view the web pages in the web browsers just by typing the address in the address bar. So in this way they transfer the data in a secure manner with the help of Intranet – the closed network.

How does data gets transferred

The data transfer from one IP host to another occurs through the Highways.

There are three different Highways, they are

- Bridges
- Routers
- Gateways

Naming Conventions

Millions of computers are connected with the net and they have to track each user connected with the net. To manage this system each user has been provided with an IP address and a password to log on to the network. The address have two parts the name and the address which is separated by @ sign. For ex. zipc214@cal2.vsnl.net.in.

This system is similar to the postal system. As each person have a name and an address by which they are identified same way with the identical Username (i.e. IP address) and password identifies a valid user.

How to connect the Net

To connect the net you require the help of an ISP. ISP the Internet Service Provider provides you the access to connect the net.

VSNL the Videsh Sanchar Nigam Ltd is one of the renowned ISP. There is lots of ISP available in the market. You can select any ISP according to your choice. For ex. Satyam, Caltiger etc. ISP provides different types of connection. They are as follows

Persistent connection

The big companies, corporate houses and different government centers uses Persistent connection. They are connected with the net for 24 hours. Though it is more costly than intermittent connections but company finds it cost effective as all the terminals of the network can log on with the same connections.

Intermittent connection/ Dial-up connection

The user using the internet for sending mail and browse the net for some time uses the Intermittent connection or you can say Dial-up connection where the user has to dial through modem and get the connection. When the user finishes the work they can disconnect. The user who uses the net for certain time finds it cheaper and if they have the time flexibility they can use the net when the phone rates are cheaper during late nights or in the early morning.

✳ ✳ ✳

2
Modems

Modem

To connect the net you first have to install a modem. There are two types of modem

- Internal Modem
- External Modem

Installation of Modem

You can select any one. In case you are using External modem its easy for you just put the jack and start installing but if you are using an Internal modem → switch off the machine → remove the cover → add the modem in one of the free PCI slot firmly

Then follow the steps and install the modem.

☛ Click on Start menu and from Settings click on Control Panel.

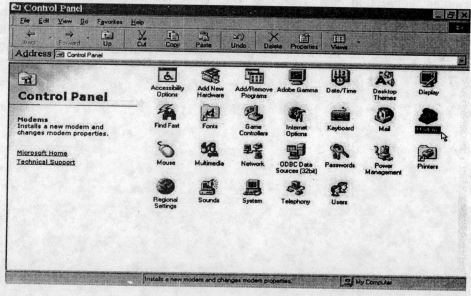

☛ Double click on the modem icon

☛ Then click on Add button

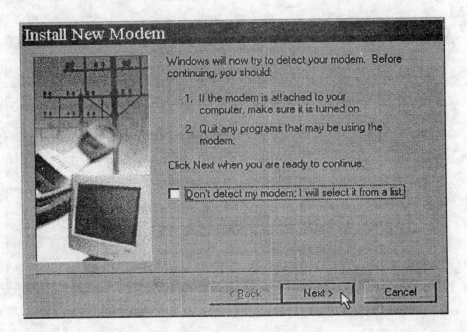

☛ Now you can ask the machine to detect the modem or if you want to detect by yourself check the option "Don't detect my modem; I will select it from a list.

• If you don't check the option the machine detects the modem and install automatically.

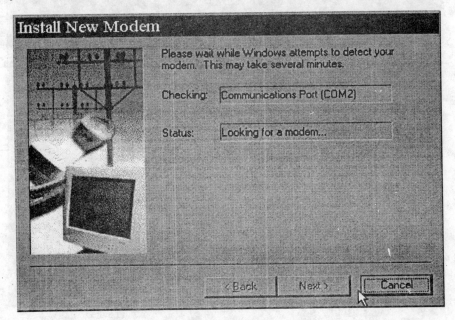

- But if you check the option you have to select the manufacturer and the model of your modem from the list. It might happen that you are not getting the modem in the list then click on Have Disk button. Insert the disk (which you have got while buying the modem).

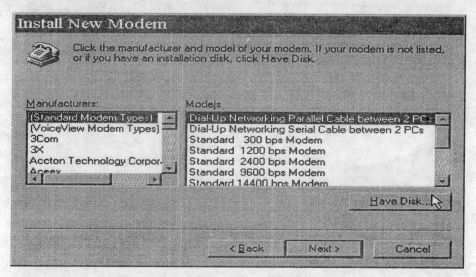

☞ Then click on Next

☞ Now you have to select the port. Select the COM port and click Next.

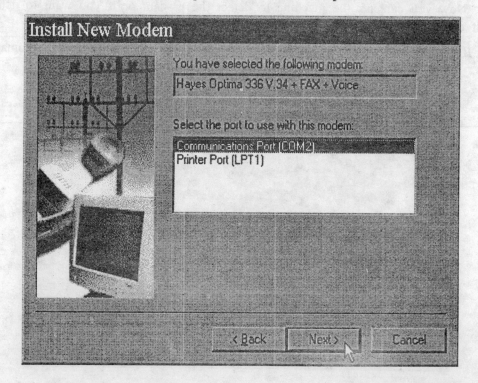

☞ Window will install the modem. Click on Finish to complete the installation.

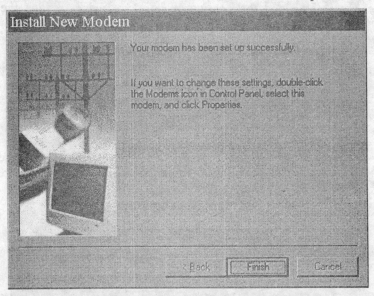

After finishing the modem installation you have to configure your PC for Internet connection. The ISP manual will guide you for the later process, which you will get while taking the connection.

How To Browse The Net

Connect the net. If you are connecting with the dial-up connection open the Auto Dialer (The view shows the VSNL auto dialer). Type the user name and the password and then click on connect.

Or click on the Launch Internet Explorer Browser icon. The dial-up connection dialog appears. Type the username and the password. Here you have to type the phone number also. Your ISP will provide you the phone numbers also.

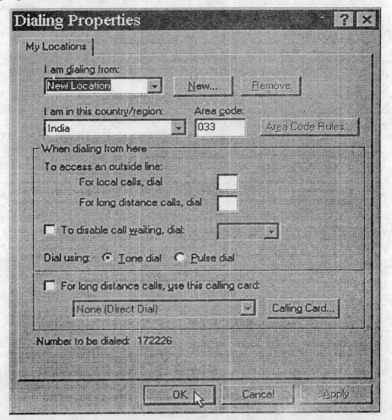

Set the properties by clicking on Dial Properties

The view shows that the system is getting connected with the network.

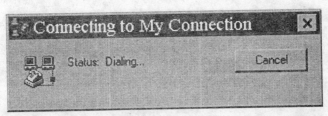

According to your ISP the Post Dial Terminal window appears. Type the user name and the password and then press F7 to continue or press continue (F7) button.

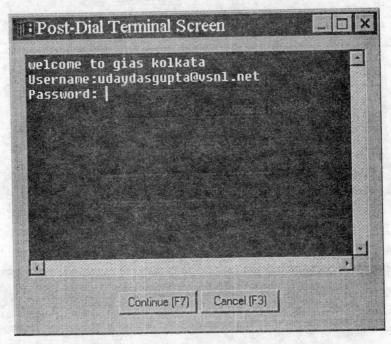

After connection you will find the connection icon in the status bar.

Then open Internet Explorer by double clicking on it. (Note-You may have any other browser say Netscape Navigator, so open your browser.)

At first the Home Page gets loaded i.e. page, which opens first is known as Home Page (For ex. You might see the msn page or you can set the Home Page according to your choice.) In the Address Bar type the web site name (say www.yahoo.com) www represents to worldwide web. Then either press Enter or click on Go. Now see the Status Bar, it shows the status of connection. It shows done after loading the page in the browser window.

Now see the yahoo.com web gets loaded in the browser.

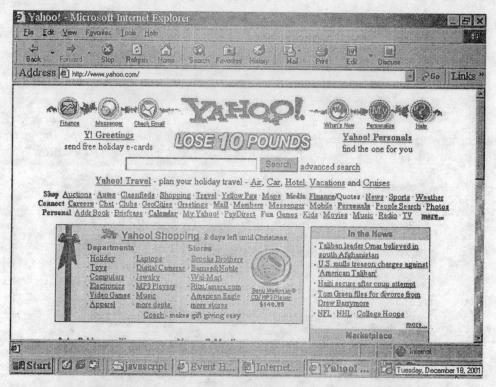

Now to load another web page type the address in the address bar again and press Enter or click on Go. For ex. Lets call the web Flowers.com

So Flowers.com web gets loaded in the browser. Repeat the same procedure to browse the net.

Working with Toolbars of Internet Explorer

Internet Explorer has three toolbars. They are as follows:

Standard Buttons. Contains the buttons necessary for browsing the net. For ex. Stop button halts loading the page in the browser.

This table will describe the details of Toolbar Icons.

Name	Description
Back	Returns you the previous visited web page.
Forward	Moves to the forward web page. (This gets enabled only if you move Back)
Stop	Stops the page from loading.
Refresh	Reloads the current document
Home	Loads the Home page. (Home page means the start page.)
Search	Opens the Search Bar, which helps in searching a web.
Favorites	Displays a list of web pages that you have added in favorites.
History	Displays the list of previously visited sites.
Full screen	Displays the view in Full screen.
Channels	Displays button for using premium web sites.
Mail	Opens the mail menu for sending and reading messages.
Print	Prints the current page.
Edit	Opens FrontPage Express for editing the web page.

Address Bar. Type a address of the site you want to visit in the address bar and then click on go or press Enter. You can directly move to a previously visited site by selecting it from the list.

Links. This toolbar takes you to useful pages. Just click on the page you want to go and it jumps to that site.

Extensions of the Web Page

As the number of web sites increased they are segregated according to their purpose.

Com   — Commercial sites

Gov   — Government sites

Org	— Organizational sites
Edu	— Educational sites
Net	— Networking sites
Mil	— Military sites

So by seeing the extensions you can identify the purpose of the sites.

How to Down Load

You can down load different objects from the net like images, software, music etc. Some web sites offer free down load facility.

Say you want to load wallpaper. Here the ex. Shown down loads wallpaper from westbengal.com web site. This site offers free down load facility.

• Select the image you want to load

• Select the size and click it.

• The wallpaper gets downloaded.

The picture appears in the desktop of your system. Later you can set the display property of the wallpaper according to your choice i.e. center, tile, stretch.

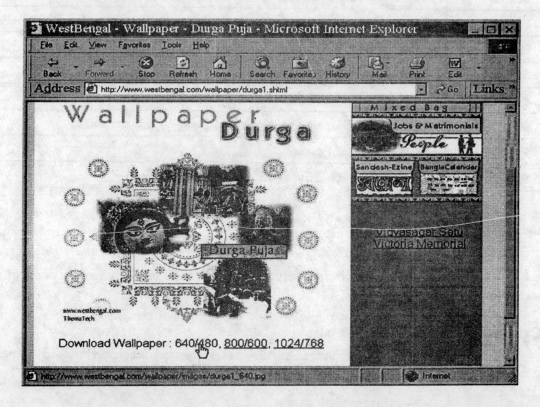

Collecting images from the Net

If you need an image from the net and you won't find the down load facility, then follow the steps

⇨ Right-click on image you want to collect

⇨ Click on Save Picture As

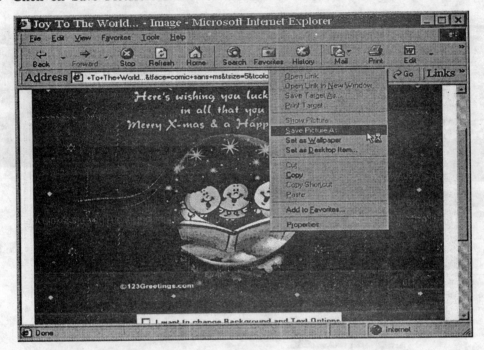

⇨The Save Picture dialog opens

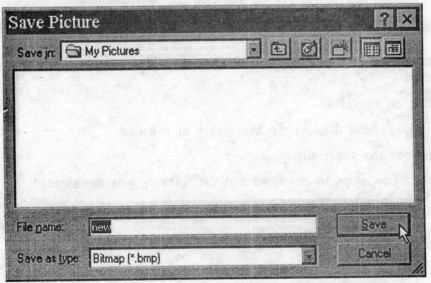

⇨ Set the location where you want to save and then click on save button. So the image gets loaded in your PC at the mentioned location.

⇨ In case you want to set the image as wallpaper after right clicking on the image click on Set as Wallpaper.

In the same way you can down load software, games etc. from the net.

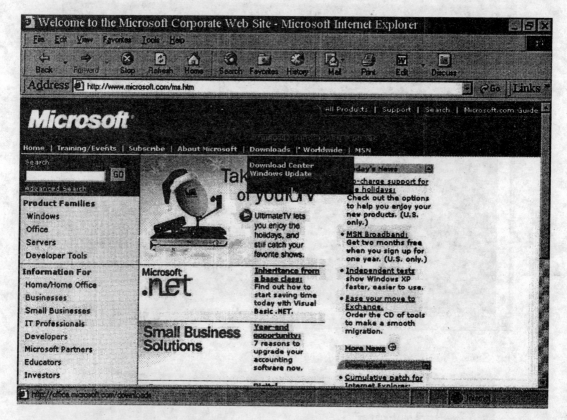

The ex. Shown displays Microsoft.com web site. This site offers software down load facility. For ex.

⇨ Click on Downloads

⇨ A popup menu displays the availability of software

⇨ Click on the one you require .

⇨ And follow steps to download and the software gets downloaded.

How to change the Home Page

Click on Start Menu → Settings → Control Panel → Internet Options

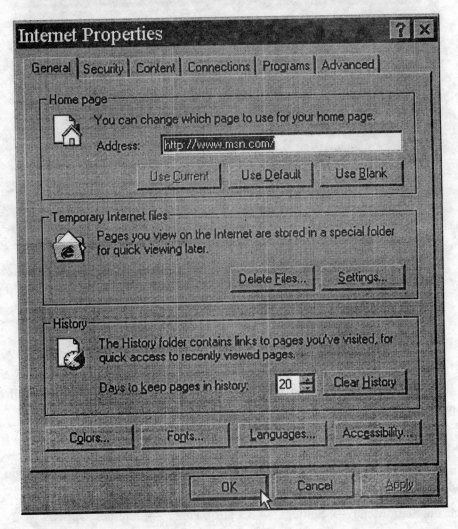

This figure shows that the home page is msn.com.

Now change the home page address to yahoo.com.

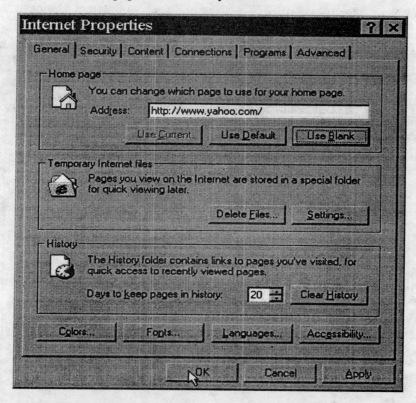

So now onwards whenever you will open the browser after connection it will open the yahoo.com page first as you have set it as home page.

How to delete Temporary Internet files

While browsing temporary files gets stored in your system. Time to time you need to delete those unnecessary files.

Click on Start Menu → Settings → Control Panel → Internet Options

Click on Delete Files.

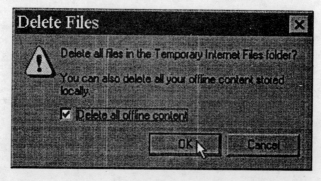

The delete files dialog appears. Check the Delete all offline content and then click OK.

Deleting files from the History folder

In the History folder you will find the list of the sites, which you have already visited. So to clear the history open General tab of Internet options by clicking on Start Menu → Settings → Control Panel → Internet Options. Then click on Clear History button.

The Internet Options dialog appears. Click on OK to delete all items in your History folder.

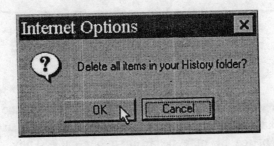

❋ ❋ ❋

3

E-mail

Introduction

The Internet users who don't have direct connections with the net (for ex. not having own PC or not having internet connections in their PC), generally uses the net from different places might be from office or may be from cyber café. They create their own e-mail address with the help of the web sites who offers e-mail facility for ex. Hotmail.com, rediff.com. These sites offer free e-mail facility just you have to create your own username and password to log on.

Users can send e-mail with the help of Outlook Express too. Generally users having their own connections use the Outlook Express to send the mail. But there is no hard and fast rule for the users, they can use any e-mail facility according to their availability and suitability.

While using the Outlook Express you can write the mail in off-line i.e. write the mail first then connect with the net and send the mail which is not possible if you are sending the mail through free mail web sites. Then you have to connect the Net first and go to the particular site. Open your e-mail using your username and password, and there you have the facility to create your mail. So when you are writing the mail you are working in on-line.

Outlook Express

Lets start with Outlook Express. Double click on the Outlook Express icon or open it from the Start Menu. It's the e-mail program, which helps you to send and receive mail. The user can write the mail in off-line and then afterwards they can send it by keeping it in outbox folder.

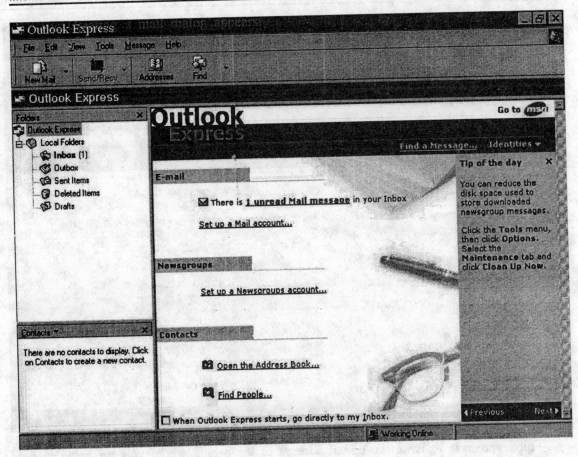

Outlook Express – folders

Inbox. Inbox folder stores the incoming mail.

Outbox. Outbox folder stores the outgoing mail.

Sent Items. Sent Items folder stores the mail, which is already sent.

Deleted Items. Deleted Items folder stores the mail, which has been deleted. If you delete from the Deleted Items folder the mail gets deleted permanently. (For ex. Same thing happens when you delete your files from Recycle Bin.)

Drafts. The mail that requires further editing, you can save those in the Drafts folder, or else you can keep a copy of the mails in the Draft folder.

How to write a mail

To start click on New Mail short cut button or you can click on File Menu → New → Mail Message.

The Creating a mail dialog appears.

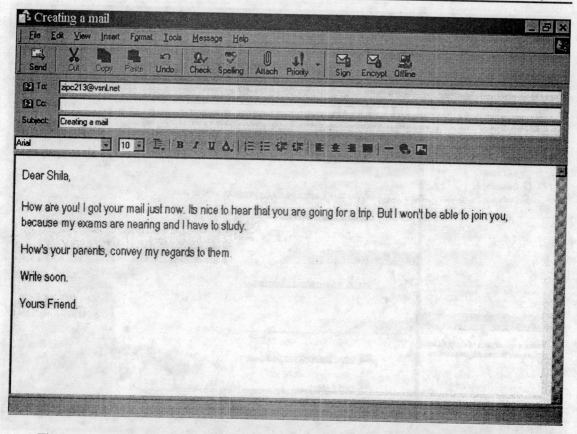

First you have to write the e-mail address of the person whom you are going to send the mail next to the **To** bar. Then write the subject of the mail, which becomes the mail title too. Now in the message area write the mail.

Here you will find all the editing facilities like changing the Font, Bold, Italic, Underline, color etc. You can use the shortcut buttons else from the Format menu click on Font. The Font dialog opens and here you find all the editing facilities.

Select the text if you have written the mail and then for editing open the Font dialog and after setting the font properties like font size, color etc click OK to make the changes permanent. You can set the Font properties before writing the mail too.

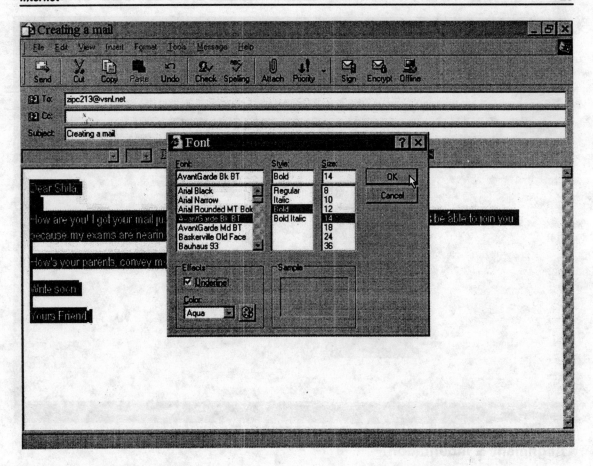

Style

You can set the Font in different style from the style short cut button or from the Format menu click on Style and select a style (For ex. To write the address you can select the address format).

You can add Bullets and Numbering either from the short cut button or by selecting the Bulleted List Style or Numbered List Style.

If required you can put a line to make an end of the mail, so you can add a horizontal line by clicking on Insert Horizontal Line shortcut button or from the Insert Menu click on Horizontal line.

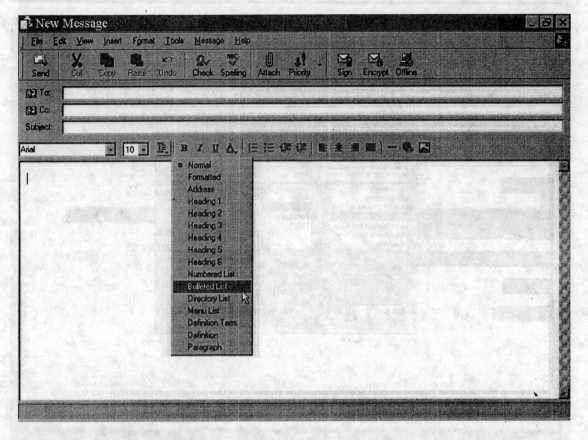

Alignment & Indentation

You can set the Alignment of the text to left, right, center or justify and can indent the text as required using the Increase Indentation and Decrease Indentation.

Adding Pictures & Background

To make your mail more attractive you can add pictures, background etc. Add picture by clicking on the Insert Picture shortcut button or from the Insert Menu. The Picture dialog opens, click on Browse and select the picture, which you want to add and click Open.

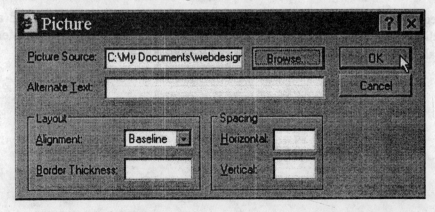

(For ex. You want to add a picture available at My Documents then after clicking on Browse, select from the Look In list My Documents, and then select the picture you want to add. Then click on Open.) Then click OK.

According to the requirement you can set the Layout like alignment, border and can set the Spacing by typing the Horizontal and Vertical values.

Background Features

You can add Background

- ☛ Color
- ☛ Picture
- ☛ Sound

To add Color click on Format Menu → Background → Color → Selected color (Say Green).

To add Picture click on Format Menu → Background → Picture → Select the File if it is available in the list else Browse and find the file → OK.

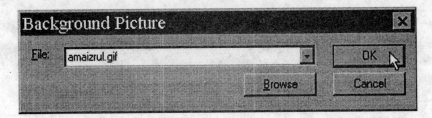

To add Sound click on Format Menu → Background → Sound → Browse the File by clicking on Browse → Set the Repeat Settings (For ex. To play the sound for a certain number say 4 times set the time property to 4 times, else select continuously to play the sound continuously.) → OK

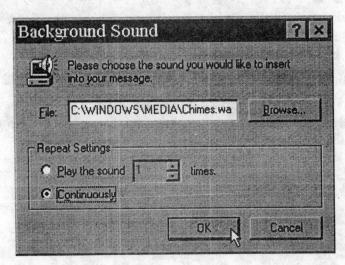

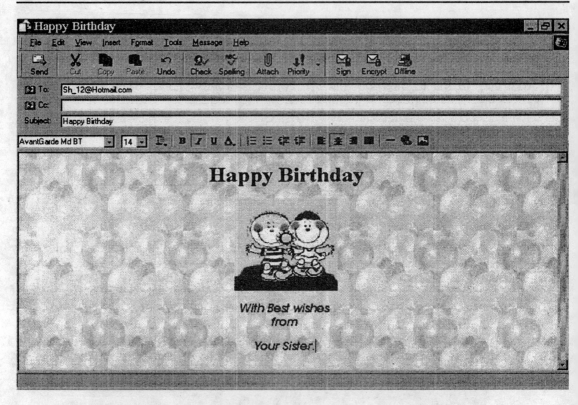

(For ex.- Created a mail by adding background, picture and sound.)

When you finish with all the editing's its time to send the mail. If you are working offline, when you click on the Send button the mail gets stored in the Outbox folder. Later after connecting with the Net open the Outbox folder by double clicking on it. It shows the list of mail you are about to sent. Select your mail double click on it, the mail opens then click on Send button.

To send and receive mails simultaneously you can use the Send/Receive button.

Creating mail by using Stationery

Adding Stationery means writing the mail by using some available formats known as Stationery.

You can select the Stationery by clicking on the downward arrow and then select Stationery from the list.

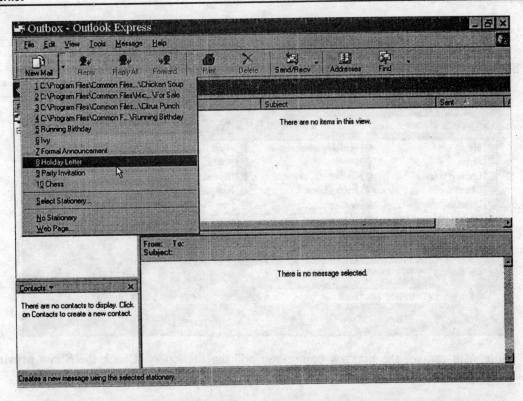

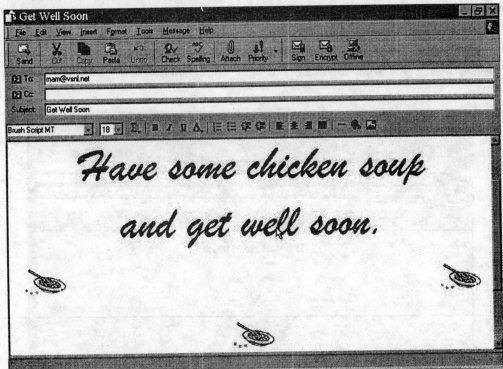

Select the stationery according to your mail subject.

In case you want to add any other Stationery, which is not available in the list click on Select Stationery. Select the Stationery that you want to add and then click OK.

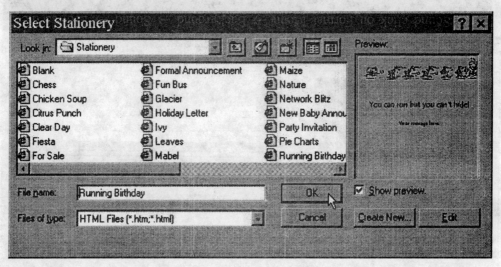

Note. You can see the preview before you add the Stationery. Check the **Show preview** to see the preview.

Attach

While sending the mail you can attach files, programs with it. So to attach files click on Attach button or from the Insert Menu you can click on File Attachment.

Select the file you want to Attach and click on Attach. Now the file gets attached with your mail.

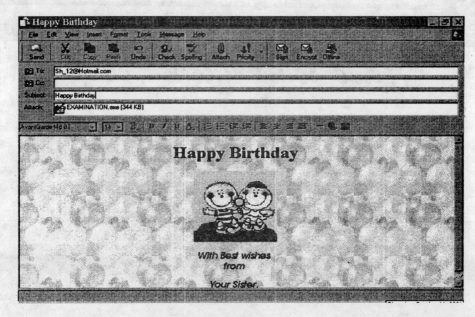

Note. I have attached a file with the mail. The Attach bar shows the file name and its size.

Address Book

The people whom you send mails can store their details in the Address Book, so that you can retrieve their e-mail address easily later on.

Click on New and then on New Contact

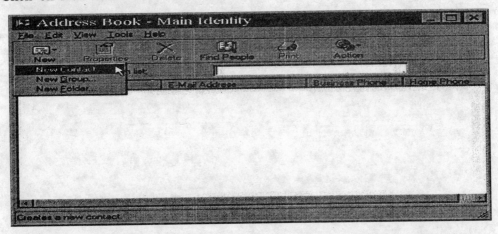

Then fill the details and click on Add to add the details in the Address Book.

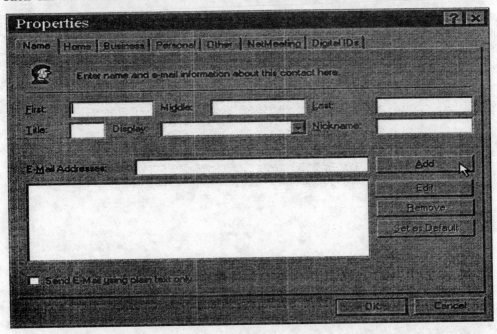

Click on each tab to fill the different information for ex. in the Home tab you can keep home related information. In this way fill all the details of each person.

HTML

HTML

4

HTML

Introduction

HTML (Hyper Text Markup Language) is used to create web pages. HTML is also known as HTML documents. Using HTML tags you can create headings, lists, bulleted list, insert picture, background, table, frames etc. The browser interprets the HTML tags and using these tag you can format the plain text to a HTML document.

While writing the code you have to use the opening tag and the closing tag. For ex. To write a HTML code

<HTML>

....

....

....

</HTML>

The / represents closing of the tag.

Working with HTML tags

Heading Tag. Heading tag begins with <H1> and ends with </H1>. You can put headings starting from <H1> to <H7>. The more you increase the heading size the headings appears smaller. Headings can be aligned to right or left by setting the <H1 align="right"> or <H1 align="left">. For aligning it centrally put the <center> tag before the heading i.e. <center><H1>........</H1></center>.

Bold tag. To make the headings or text bold you should start with <B> and ends with </B>.

Italics tag. Similarly for setting the text or headings in an italic format use the italics tag i.e. it should start from <I> and ends with </I>.

Underline tag . For adding an underline use the underline tags i.e. it should start from <U> and ends with </U>.

Paragraph tag. To begin a paragraph you should start with <P> and it should end with </P> tag.

Big tag. The Big tag begins with <Big> and ends with </Big>. Text enclosed within the Big tag appears bigger in size.

Small tag. The Small tag begins with <Small> and ends with </Small>. Text enclosed within the Small tag appears smaller in size.

Superscript tag. The superscript tag begins with ^{tag and ends with} tag. The text enclosed inside the superscript tag appears in a superscript format. For ex. To write a date 31st write st to get the superscript effect.

Subscript tag. The subscript tag begins with _{tag and ends with} tag. The text enclosed inside the superscript tag appears in a superscript format. For ex. To write X_1 write ₁ to get the subscript effect.

Writing the code

Open Notepad by clicking on the Start menu ☞ Programs ☞ Accessories ☞ Notepad Write the code and then save it with an .html or .htm extension.

Note. See the editor view given below.

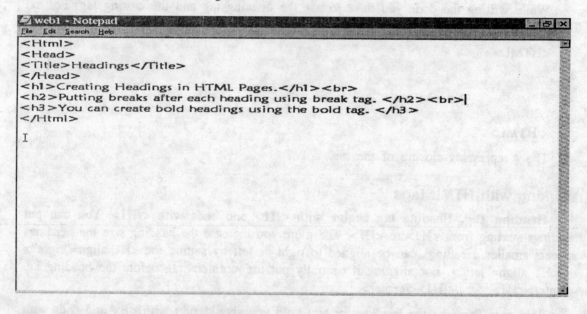

```
web1 - Notepad
File  Edit  Search  Help
<Html>
<Head>
<Title>Headings</Title>
</Head>
<h1>Creating Headings in HTML Pages.</h1><br>
<h2>Putting breaks after each heading using break tag. </h2><br>|
<h3>You can create bold headings using the bold tag. </h3>
</Html>

I
```

The Browser View

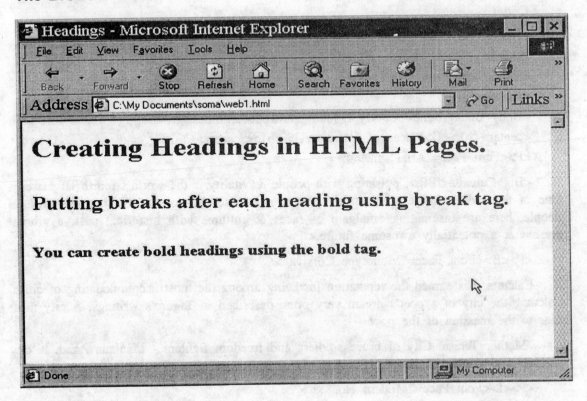

Working with Background

So now you have got a preliminary idea of creating web pages. Lets make it colorful by putting background.

For adding a background color the syntax is <Body Bgcolor="yellow"> This will add yellow color in the body of the HTML document. You can set any color according to your choice.

Similarly to add a background picture in the body of the HTML document, first select the picture you want add.

Then write the syntax.

<Body Background="C:\My Documents\webdesign\background.jpg">

While writing you have to write the picture file name with its extension and you have to mention its source.

In this ex. Picture file name is background.

Extension of the file is jpg, and the source of the files C:\My Documents\webdesign, and the source is separated by \.

Follow the code, which adds a background in a HTML document.

Code:

```
<Html>
<Head>
<Title>Background</Title>
</Head>
<Body Background="C:\My Documents\webdesign\background.jpg" Text="Red">
<center><h1><U>Places of Interest</U></h1></center>
<P><Font Face="Arial" size=4>
```

<Big>Calcutta</Big>, pulsating with people & vitality is the world's fourth largest city. One of the India's biggest industrial centres, it is also the core of the nation's culture. People, here are fascinating amalgam of races & cultures with historical past, a vibrant present & a potentially awesome future.</P>

<P><B><Font Face="Monotype Corsiva">

Calcutta, has earned the reputation for being among the most accommodating of cities. Calcutta, the city of a poet's dream very often described in Tagore's writings. A city most dear to the messiah of the poor –

 Mother Teresa. City of brave soldiers and freedom fighters - Maulana Azad. A city of trade and commerce and truly a city of joy and hope.</B></P>

<P><I><Font Face="Modern No. 20">

<Small>Today, at the brink of the 21st century, Calcutta is poised on the verge of another change. Trade and commerce is picking up, with the changing lifestyles and economic boom our beloved Calcutta continues to enchant, in its vibrant shades, encompassing all facets of life & livelihood.</Small><I><P>

```
<br>
<HR Color="Blue">
```

<Address>To Visit Calcutta and for more details contact West Bengal Toursim Department.</Address>

```
</Body>
</Html>
```

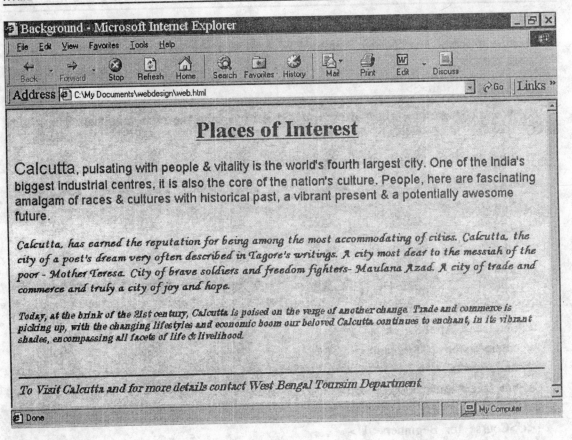

HR tag

<HR> tag adds a horizontal line. The color is changed according to your choice. The syntax for changing the color is <HR color="blue">

Address tag

<Address> tag is mainly used to write address. It begins with <Address> and ends with </Address>. The address tag makes the text italic.

Creating List

Now lets create a list. You can create Ordered list, Unordered list and Definition Term.

Ordered List. You can create ordered list by putting the <Ol> tag and create the list by putting <Li> tag for each item.

For ex.
<Ol>
<Li>Windows 98
<Li>Ms Office 2000
<Li>Internet
</Ol>

This will create an ordered list. But sometime it may happen that you need to start the list from a different number say 3 instead of 1 so you can solve that problem by setting the start number.

<Ol type=1 Start=3>

You can change the format of the ordered list by using the type command. The syntax is <Ol type=I>. So now the list will appear as I, II, III.

Follow the code, which creates an ordered list.

Code:

```
<Html>
<Head>
<Title>Creating List</Title>
</Head>
<Body Bgcolor="pink" Text="blue">
<Font size=5>
<Font face="Arial Black">
<center>Vision 2000</center>
<Font size=3>
<Font face="Lucida Fax">
<P>
<U>Course for Beginners</U>
<Ol>
<Li>Windows 98
<Li>Ms Office 2000
<Li>Internet
</Ol>
</P>
<P>
<U>Programming Course</U>
<Ol type=1 start=4>
<Li>C++
<Li>Visual Basic
<Li>Java 2.0
<Li>Foxpro 2.6
</Ol>
</P>
<P>
<U>Web Designing</U>
```

```
<Ol type=I>
<Li>Internet Concepts
<Li>Html
<Li>Dhtml
</Ol>
</P>
</Body>
</Html>
```

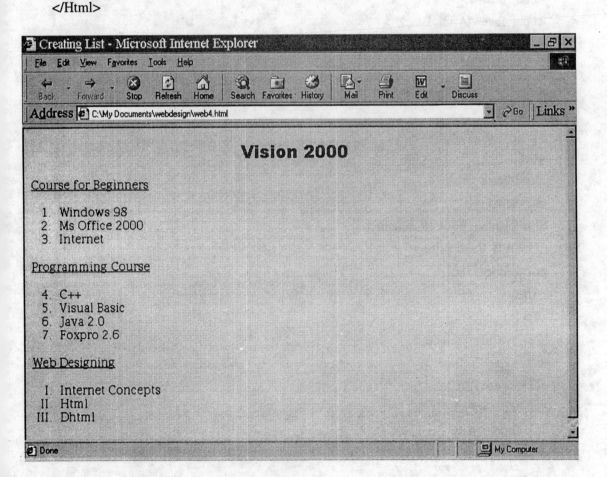

Unordered List. For creating a bulleted list you have to create an Unordered list. Unordered list begins with the <Ul> tag and to represent the list item you have to use the <Li> tag. The bullet appears in front of each item. You can change the style by setting the Type of the bullets. By default it appears round. Say to change its shape to square you have to set the Type="Square".

Follow the code, which creates an unordered list.

Code:

```
<Html>
<Head>
<Title>Creating List</Title>
</Head>
<Body Bgcolor="pink" Text="blue">
<Font size=5>
<Font face="Arial Black">
<center>Book Shop</center>
<Font size=3>
<Font face="Lucida Fax">
<P>
<U>List of Publishers</U>
<Ul>
<Li>Microsoft
<Li>Sams
<Li>Khanna Book Publications
<Li>BPB Publications
<Li>Pentice Hall
</UL>
</P>
Now we also sell<Br>
<UL type="square">
<Li>Mouse
<Li>Mouse Pad
<Li>Games Cds
</Ul>
</P>
</Body>
</Html>
```

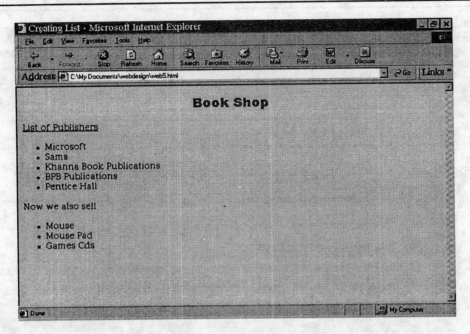

Definition List. Definition list starts with <Dl> tag and ends with </Dl>. It includes <Dt> tag i.e. Definition Term and <DD> tag i.e. Definition Description. Generally you use this list where a description is required for each term.

Follow the code, which creates a definition list.

Code:

```
<Html>
<Head>
<Title>Creating List</Title>
</Head>
<Body Bgcolor="yellow" Text="red">
<Font size=5>
<Font face="Lucida Fax">
<center>Software Details</center>
<Font size=4>
<P>
<Dl>
<Dt>Windows 98
<DD>Operating System
<Dt>Ms Word 2000
<DD>Word processor
<Dt>Ms Excel 2000
<DD>Spreadsheet package
</Dl>
</P>
</Body>
</Html>
```

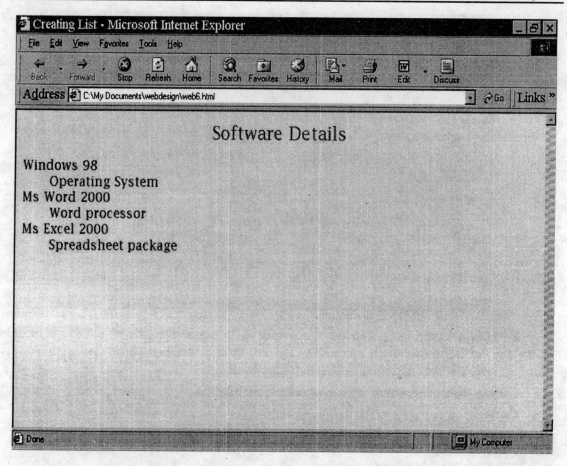

This page displays the feature of Definition list. First comes the term i.e. Windows 98 and then the definition Operating System.

✳ ✳ ✳

5

Working with Images

Image makes the web pages more impressive. You can add an image using the <img> tag. Then you have to write the source of the file with the filename and with its extension name like jpg, gif, bmp etc.

How to search images?

Using the find files option you can search files by putting the name or extension name. Suppose you want to find the list of available jpg files in your PC. So follow these steps

⇨ Click on Start Menu

⇨ Find

⇨ Files or Folders, the Find dialog appears

⇨ In the Named text box type the extension as *.jpg

⇨ Then from the look in list select the drive. For ex. To search from the hard disk select the C drive i.e. your hard disk drive.

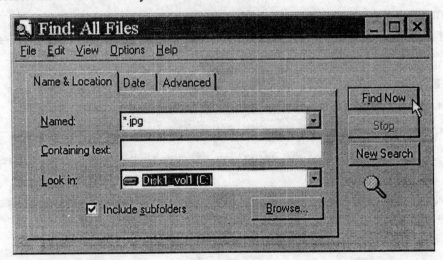

⇨ After selecting click on Find Now and it will give you the list of jpg files available in your PC with its source, size, type and the modified date and time. To get all these information set the view of the Find dialog to Details view. Other views will the display the file name only in different format.

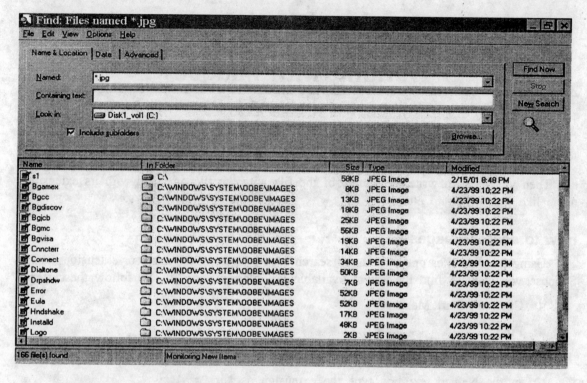

So now find out which image you want to add and its source and mention the source in the image tag to drop the image in the web page.

Adding images and handling its attributes

To add an image you have to mention its source. For ex: <img Src="c:\my documents\web\flower1.jpg">

Src represents the source of the file.

Height. Sets the image height. For ex. height="100".

Width. Sets the image width. For ex. width="100".

Align. Sets the alignment of the image. For ex. img align="right", here img represents image.

Follow the code, which explains how to call images and its other attributes, like height, width, align etc.

Code :

```
<Html>
<Head>
<Title>Images</Title>
</Head>
<Body background="C:\My Documents\webdesign\sun.jpg" Text="Black">
<Font Face="Lucida Handwriting">
<Font size=9>
<center>Flower</center>
<Font Face="Modern No. 20">
<Font size=4>
<img align="Left" width="100" height="100" src="C:\My
Documents\webdesign\flower3.jpg">
```

<P>Flowers are symbolic of beauty, love and tranquility. They form the soul of a garden and convey the message of nature to man. In our country, flowers are sanctified and are commonly used in worship in homes and temples. We are intimately associated with flowers and on all festive occasions, marriages, religious ceremonies and social functions; the use of flowers and garlands has become almost essential. So the importance for flower cultivation is also increasing.</P>

```
<img align="right" width="100" height="100" src="C:\My
Documents\webdesign\rose1.gif">
```

<P>

Besides their aesthetic value, flowers are also important for their economic value. Cut flowers, extraction of perfumes etc have great market demand. An earlier survey made by the Indian Council of Agricultural Research has revealed that about 10500 tons of cut flowers worth Rs9.26 crores are sold annually in the markets of metropolitan cities like Bombay, Calcutta, Madras, Delhi.</P>

```
</Body>
</Html>
```

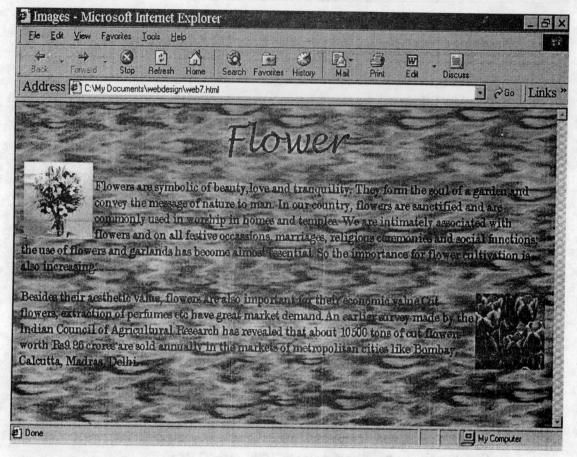

Other image attributes

Border. We can put borders around the image by setting the border width. For ex. border=2.

Hspace . Using this attribute you can set the horizontal spacing to be left while placing the image. For ex. Hspace="50".

Vspace. Using this attribute you can set the vertical spacing to be left while placing the image. For ex. Vspace="50".

Follow the code, which explains how to put image border and other attributes like Hspace,Vspace etc.

Code :

```
<Html>

<Head>

<Title>Images</Title>

</Head>

<Body Background="c:\my documents\webdesign\pink.jpg">

<img width=100 height=100 Border=2 Hspace=50 Src="C:\My
Documents\webdesign\rose5.gif">

<img width=100 height=100 Border=2 Hspace=65 Src="C:\My
Documents\webdesign\rabbit.gif">

<img width=100 height=100 Border=2 Hspace=80 Src="C:\My
Documents\webdesign\gift8.jpg">

<Font size=6>

<center>Gift Items</center>

<Font size=4>

<img align="left" width=100 height=100 Border=3 Src="C:\My
Documents\webdesign\doll.gif">

This doll hops and sings a nice song.<Br>Now a special discount of Rs.100. <Br>The
price is Rs.1000.<Br><Br><Br><Br><Br>

<img align="left" width=100 height=100 Border=3 Src="C:\My
Documents\webdesign\rose3.gif">

A bunch of rose, red in color, beautiful smell.<Br> One dozen flowers cost Rs.100.

<A href="C:\My Documents\webdesign\web9.html">

<Br><Br><Br><Br><Br><Br><Br><Br>

<Img border="0" align="right" src="C:\Program Files\Microsoft Visual
Studio\Common\Graphics\Icons\Arrows\Arw06rt.ico"></A>

<A href="C:\My Documents\webdesign\web7.html">

<Img border="0" align="right" src="C:\Program Files\Microsoft Visual
Studio\Common\Graphics\Icons\Arrows\Arw06lt.ico"></A>

</Body>

</Html>
```

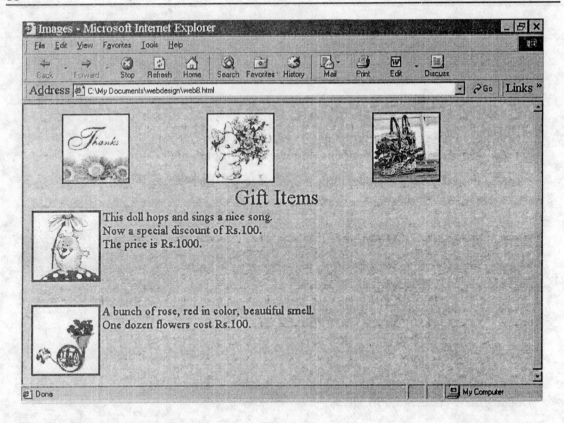

Working with dynamic image

Now lets add dynamic image and sounds in the web page. This will make your web page more attractive. For adding moving image (For ex. avi files) you have to use the <img> tag following with the DnySrc (Dynamic Source) of the file. Further you have mention the loop times i.e. how many times it will run after getting loaded in the browser. Here if you say Loop="infinite" then it runs continuously and if you mention Loop="5" then it works only for five times. So if you set the times it will run according to that.

How to search dynamic image files?

Using the find files option you can search dynamic image files by putting the name or extension name. Suppose you want to find the list of available avi files in your PC. So follow these steps

⇨ Click on Start Menu
⇨ Find
⇨ Files or Folders, the Find dialog appears
⇨ In the Named text box type the extension as *.avi
⇨ Then from the look in list select the drive. For ex. To search from the hard disk select the C drive i.e. your hard disk drive.

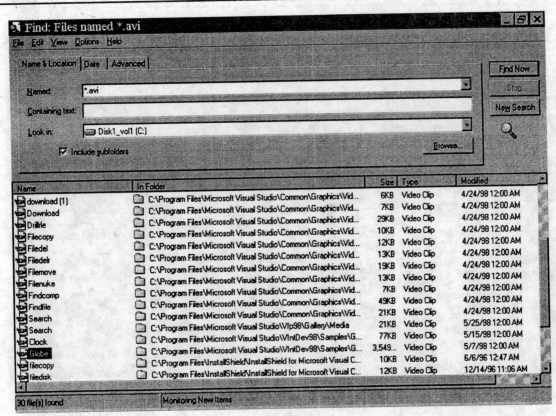

⇨ After selecting click on Find Now and it will give you the list of avi files available in your PC with its source, size, type and the modified date and time. To get all these information set the view of the Find dialog to Details view. Other views will the display the file name only in different format. Then select the file according to your requirement.

Follow the code, which explains how to add dynamic image.

Code:

```
<Html>
<Head>
<Title>Moving Pictures</Title>
</Head>
<Body Bgcolor="sky blue">
<Center><img width=300 height=250 loop="infinite" dynsrc="C:\Program
Files\Microsoft Visual
Studio\VIntdev98\samples\Gallery\content\mmedia\Globe.avi"><Br>
</Center>
</Body>
</Html>
```

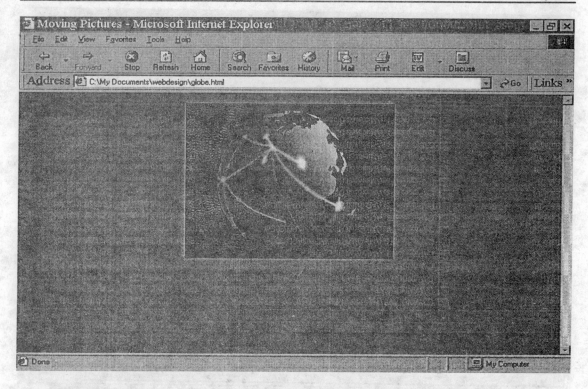

After the page gets loaded in the browser you will find a globe moving continuously. It might happen that this image is not available in your machine you can add any image according to your choice and availability.

Adding Background Sound

You can add sounds too in the web page. Lets add background sound. You have to use the <Bgsound> following with the Src(Source) of the file.

<Body Bgsound Src="sound.mid" Loop="infinite"> The sound gets added in the body of the web.Loop=infinite plays the sound continuously. Whereas if you set the Loop=1 then it plays the sound once after the page gets loaded in the browser.

How to search sound files?

Using the find files option you can search sound files by putting the name or extension name. Suppose you want to find the list of available mid or wav files in your PC. So follow these steps

    ⇒ Click on Start Menu

    ⇒ Find

    ⇒ Files or Folders, the Find dialog appears

    ⇒ In the Named text box type the extension as *.mid

⇨ Then from the look in list select the drive. For ex. To search from the hard disk select the C drive i.e. your hard disk drive.

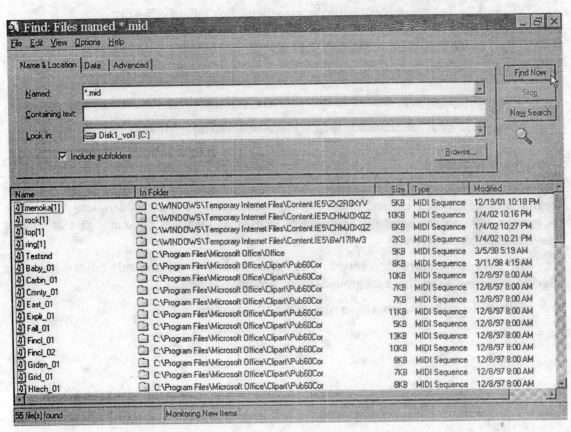

⇨ After selecting click on Find Now and it will give you the list of mid files available in your PC with its source, size, type and the modified date and time. To get all these information set the view of the Find dialog to Details view. Other views will the display the file name only in different format.

Select a sound according to your choice and add the sound as background sound in your web page.

Follow the code, which shows the effect of background sound.

Code :

```
<Html>
<Head>
<Title>Moving Pictures</Title>
</Head>
<Body Bgcolor="sky blue">
<Bgsound src="C:\Program Files\Microsoft Office\Clipart\Pub60Cor\Grden_01.mid"
Loop="infinite">
```

```
<Center><img width=300 height=250 loop="infinite" dynsrc="C:\Program
Files\Microsoft Visual
Studio\VIntdev98\samples\Gallery\content\mmedia\Globe.avi"><Br>
</Center>
</Body>
</Html>
```

When this page gets loaded in the browser you can hear the background sound.

Note. Hardware requirements to get the sound facility – Sound card & sound box.

Adding Marquee

Text included within the <marquee> tag moves continuously from right to left. Marquee begins with <Marquee> tag and ends with the </Marquee>. For ex. <Marquee> The Globe is moving. </Marquee>. Actually <Marquee> is used to highlight the message that catches the attention of the users.

To make it more attractive you can add a background color.<Marquee Bgcolor="yellow"> so the background color becomes yellow.

Follow the code, which shows the effect of marquee.

Code :

```
<Html>
<Head>
<Title>Moving Pictures</Title>
</Head>
<Body Bgcolor="sky blue">
<Bgsound src="C:\Program Files\Microsoft Office\Clipart\Pub60Cor\Grden_01.mid"
Loop="infinite">
<Center><img width=300 height=250 loop="infinite" dynsrc="C:\Program
Files\Microsoft Visual
Studio\VIntdev98\samples\Gallery\content\mmedia\Globe.avi"><Br>
<Font size=9>
Globe
</Center>
<Marquee Bgcolor="yellow">The Globe is moving</Marquee>
</Body>
</Html>
```

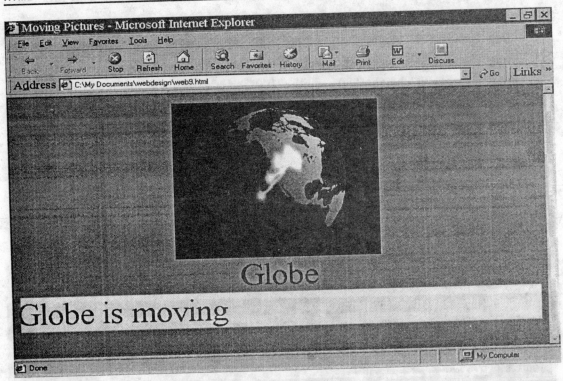

* Now this web page shows all the three HTML tags i.e. calling a dynamic image, putting background sound and marquee.

Creating marquee using pictures

Instead of text you can add image too as a marquee. <Marquee><img src="doll.gif"</Marquee> this will load the picture and it will work as a marquee.

Lets create a web using images inside the marquee instead of text.

Follow the code, which shows marquee of images

Code :

```
<Html>
<Head>
<Title>Moving Pictures</Title>
</Head>
<Body>
<Font size=9>
<Center><H1>Creating marquee with pictures</H1>
</Center>
<Br><Br>
```

```
<Marquee>
<img Hspace="5" height="80" width="100" src="C:\My Documents\nature1.jpg">
<img Hspace="5" height="80" width="100" src="C:\My Documents\fuji.jpg">
<img Hspace="5" height="80" width="100" src="C:\My Documents\garden.jpg">
<img Hspace="5" height="80" width="100" src="C:\My Documents\nature2.jpg">
<img Hspace="5" height="80" width="100" src="C:\My Documents\spring.jpg">
<img Hspace="5" height="80" width="100" src="C:\My Documents\windmill.jpg">
<img Hspace="5" height="80" width="100" src="C:\My Documents\vidsetu_thumb.jpg">
<img Hspace="5" height="80" width="100" src="C:\My Documents\fish.jpg">
</Marquee>
</Body>
</Html>
```

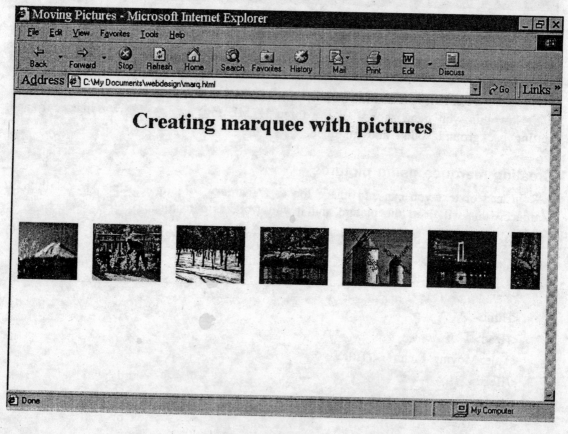

✻ ✻ ✻

6
Forms

When you are going to handle data, you require Textbox, Text area, Listbox, Combobox, Checkbox etc. These are all Form elements. So lets create Form, first study the list of Form elements.

Form elements

Textbox. Handles the text field of the Form.

Password. Handles the password field of the Form.

Text area. Handles the text area field of Form. It is mainly used for handling larger text. For ex. address field.

Radio. Handles the radio button of the Form. You can handle a set of radio buttons or an individual radio button.

Check box. Handles the check box of the Form.

Select. Handles the select list of the Form. When the size of the select list is not mentioned it works like a combo box.

Option. This object handles the elements of the list of a Form.

Button. Handles the button of the Form.

Submit button. Handles the submit button of the Form.

Reset button. Handles the reset button of the Form.

So now lets create a Form by adding this Form elements.

Lets create a Form where the user had to type their name, password, address, and they can select their areas of interest.

For the name field you require a textbox. You can add a textbox by setting the input tag as <Input type="text" size=40> size will set the size of the textbox.

To add a password field you have to mention the input type as password, say <Input type="password" size=10>

Address field requires more space so it is ideal to add a textarea for the address field. Textarea begins with the <Textarea> tag and ends with </Textarea> proceeding with the number of rows and columns.

Next I have added a Combobox, which shows the list of all cities so that user can select any of them from the list. To create a Combobox you have to start with the <Select> tag and it ends with the </Select>. Each option you want to add begins with the <Option> tag.

At the end of this page the user are asked to select the Areas of Interest.

For this you have to use Checkbox before each item. To add Checkbox you have to use the <Input> tag and mention the Type as Checkbox.

Now follow the code, which displays all these Form elements.

Code :

```
<Html>
<Head>
<Title>Creating Forms</Title>
</Head>
<Body Bgcolor="Gold" Text="Red">
<Font size=6>
<Center>Creating Forms</Center>
<Br>
<Font size=5>
Enter your Name <Input type="Name" size=40><Br><Br>
Enter your Password <Input type="Password" size=10><Br><Br>
Enter your Address <Textarea name="Address" rows=4 cols=20></Textarea><Br><Br>
Select your city<Select>
<Option>Kolkata
<Option>Agra
<Option>Delhi
<Option>Chennai
<Option>Bangalore
<Option>hyderabad
<Option>Chandigarh
</Select><Br><Br>
Select your Areas of Interest<Br>
<input type="Checkbox">Music
<input type="Checkbox">Games
```

```
<input type="Checkbox">Books
<input type="Checkbox">Cds
<input type="Checkbox">Dance
<input type="Checkbox">Computer
<input type="Checkbox">Business
<input type="Checkbox">Cricket
</Body>
</Html>
```

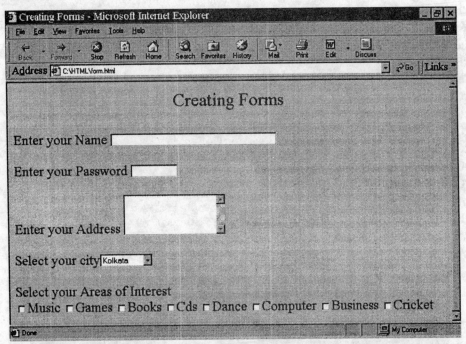

Now lets add the other controls like radio buttons, List box and buttons. Radio button is ideal where the users have to select any of the option. So here in this example radio button is used for selecting the gender (Male or Female). Creation of radio button begins with the <Input> tag following with the type as Radio. Then you have put a name for the name attribute and make it as on. <Input Type="Radio" name=R1="on">

Set the name same for all the radio buttons you are adding, so that only one option gets selected.

Then to add List box you have to mention the size and according to the size mentioned list options are visible. For ex. If you set the List box size as 4 then 4 options will be visible, to view the other options you have to scroll down.

Another feature is adding buttons. Though in HTML you cannot add the functionality but you can create it. You can add the button using the input tag mentioning the type as button. You can set the value according to your choice. For ex. <Input type= "Button" value= "Thankyou"> so this adds the button in the form and changes its value.

Code :

```
<Html>
<Head>
<Title>Creating Forms</Title>
</Head>
<Body Bgcolor="Gold" Text="Red">
<Font size=6>
<Center>More Information</Center>
<Br>
<Font size=5>
You are a <Input type="Radio" name=r1="on">Male <Input type="Radio"
name=r1="on">Female
<Br><Br>
Select the food you like most<Select size=4>
<Option>Sweets
<Option>Cakes
<Option>Pizzas
<Option>Juice
<Option>Soup
<Option>Fruits
</Select><Br><Br>
<Input type="Button" Value="Thankyou">
</Body>
</Html>
```

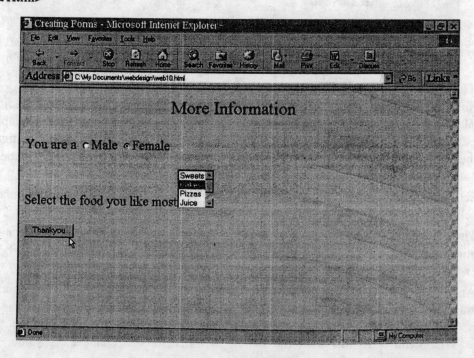

7

Tables

To display data on the web page you need to create tables. For creating tables you have to use the <Table> tag following with the <Tr> and <Td>. The Border attribute creates a border according to the thickness mentioned. In case you want to avoid the border then write it as 0. <Table Border=0>

Working with the table tags

<Tr> tag. <Tr> tag means starting of a table row, whereas </Tr> means end of a Table row.

<Th> tag. <Th> tag creates the table heading, which appears in a bold format. At the end of each heading close it with </Th>.

<Td> tag. <Td> tag means starting of the Table data, whereas </Td> means end of a Table data.

You can set the alignment of the table data too. For ex. <Td align="left"> So the data will be left aligned.

Follow the code of this page where a table has been created using the <Tr> and <Td> tag.

Code :

```
<Html>
<Head>
<Title>Tables</Title>
</Head>
<Body Bgcolor="green" Text="yellow">
<Font Face="Arial Black">
<Font size=5>
<Center>Creating Tables
<Br><Br><Br>
```

```
<Font size=4>
<Table border=1>
<Tr>
<Th>Roll-No</Th><Th>Marks</Th><Th>Grade</Th>
</Tr>
<Tr>
<Td>A001</Td><Td>600</Td><Td align="center">B</Td>
</Tr>
<Tr>
<Td>A002</Td><Td>670</Td><Td align="center">A</Td>
</Tr>
</Table>
</Center>
</Body>
</Html>
```

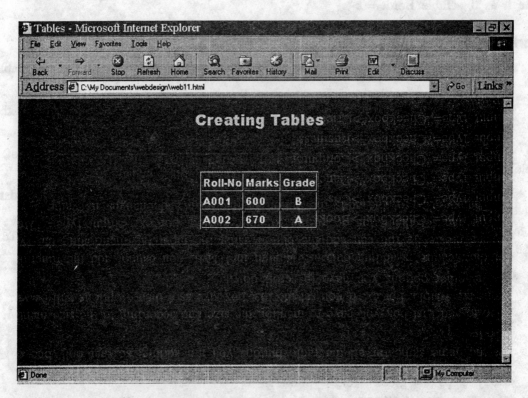

As because the Table data alignment is mentioned as center for the data of Grade column so the data "B" and "A" appears centrally.

If required you can align the total row also. That is shown in the next example.

Cellspacing

In this step you will learn the other features of table. Say you have noticed one problem that the width of the cell depends upon the text. To make all the cells equal, for a better appearance of the table cellspacing is used.

<Table border=3 color="red" cellspacing=8 width=35% align="center">

Here the border width is increased to 3, which gives a 3d effect.

According to your requirement set the width percentage.

Here all the data has been aligned centrally because it is mentioned the table align as center.

Another feature is Bgcolor. <Th Bgcolor="Blue"> this makes the background color blue of the table heading.

Here the bgcolor of the table data is changed. <Td Bgcolor="orange">

Follow the code, which shows the effect of Cellspacing.

Code :

```
<Html>
<Head>
<Title>Tables</Title>
</Head>
<Body Bgcolor="green" Text="yellow">
<Font Face="Arial Black">
<Font size=5>
<Center>CELLSPACING
<Br><Br><Br>
<Font size=4>
<Table border=3 color="red" cellspacing=8 width=35% align="center">
<Tr>
<Th    Bgcolor="Blue">Roll-No</Th><Th    Bgcolor="Blue">Marks</Th><Th
Bgcolor="Blue">Grade</Th>
</Tr>
<Tr align="center">
<Td    Bgcolor="Orange">A001</Td><Td    Bgcolor="Orange">600</Td><Td
Bgcolor="Orange">B</Td>
</Tr>
<Tr align="center">
<Td    Bgcolor="Orange">A002</Td><Td    Bgcolor="Orange">670</Td><Td
Bgcolor="Orange">A</Td>
</Tr>
</Table>
</Center>
</Body>
</Html>
```

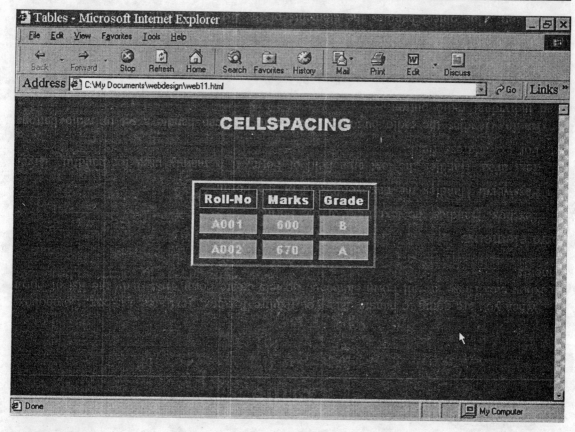

Cellpadding

Another feature is Cellpadding. <Table border=1 color="red" cellpadding=10 width=35% align="center">

This makes all the rows and columns equal. Other attributes like Bgcolor, border etc are same as Cellspacing.

Follow the code, which shows Cellpadding.

Code :

```
<Html>
<Head>
<Title>Tables</Title>
</Head>
<Body Bgcolor="green" Text="yellow">
<Font Face="Arial Black">
<Font size=5>
<Center>CELLPADDING
<Br><Br><Br>
```

```
<Font size=4>
<Table border=1 color="red" Ceilpadding=10 width=35% align="center">
<Tr>
<Th>Roll-No</Th><Th>Marks</Th><Th>Grade</Th>
</Tr>
<Tr>
<Td>A001</Td><Td>600</Td><Td align="center">B</Td>
</Tr>
<Tr>
HTML
<Td>A002</Td><Td>670</Td><Td align="center">A</Td>
</Tr>
</Table>
</Center>
</Body>
</Html>
```

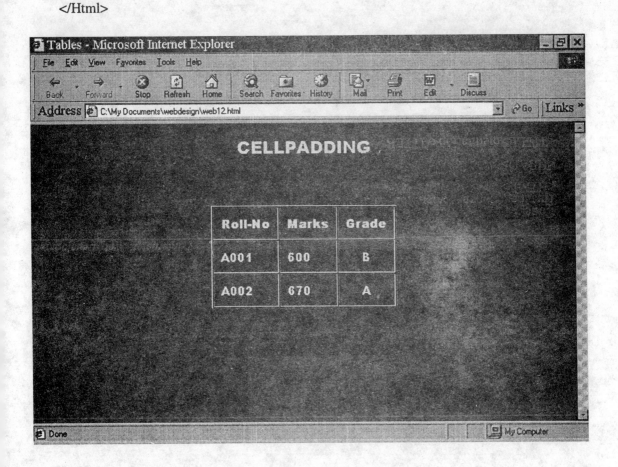

Rowspan & Colspan

You can increase the rows and columns size according to your need using the rowspan and colspan tag. Using these tags you can create the table in your own structured format.

Follow the code, which shows the use of Rowspan & Colspan.

The table shows the Roll no. of students and the marks obtained in each Term.

Code :

```
<Html>
<Head>
<Title>Tables</Title>
</Head>
<Body Bgcolor="cream" text="red">
<center><h2>Rowspan & Colspan</h2></center><br><br>
<Table Border=3 align="center">
<Tr>
<Th Rowspan=2>Roll-No</Th>
<Th Colspan=3>Marks</Th>
<Th Rowspan=2>Term</Th>
</Tr>
<Tr>
<Th>English</Th>
<Th>Maths</Th>
<Th>Computer</Th>
</Tr>
<Tr>
<Td Rowspan=2>A001</Td><Td>70</Td><Td>78</Td>
<Td>80</Td><Td >1st</Td>
</Tr>
<Tr>
<Td>87</Td><Td>65</Td><Td>82</Td><Td >2nd</Td>
</Tr>
</Table>
</Body>
</Html>
```

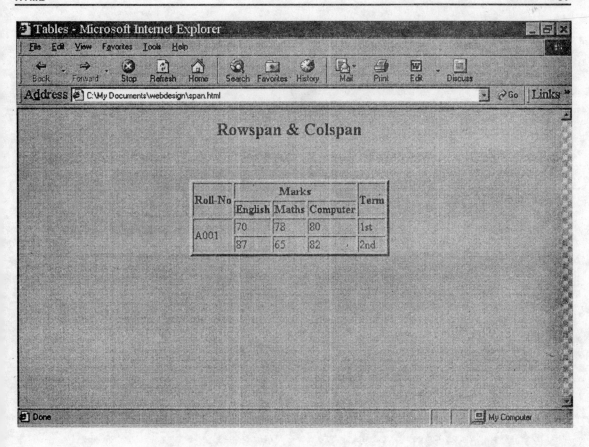

✳ ✳ ✳

8

Links

Now we will create links. Links help you to move to other sites in a single click. Usually link contains the reference of the other sites. It begins with a <A Href="filename.html"> tag and ends with </A>. You can create link on text or on images too.

Now study the code of this web page where links are created on the text.

Code :

```
<HTML>
<HEAD>
<TITLE>HYPERLINK</TITLE>
</HEAD>
<BODY bgcolor="gold" text="red">
<FONT FACE="MONOTYPE CORSIVA">
<H2><CENTER>OLD AGE HOME</CENTER></H2><BR>
<font size=5>
Come and share your old days with us and forget your all tensions. Enjoy with
different types of entertainment we have made for you.
<img align="right" src="C:\Program Files\Common Files\Microsoft
Shared\Clipart\cagcat50\Bd06639_.wmf">
Here you will find
<ol>
<li><a href="C:\My Documents\webdesign\Library.HTML">Library</a>
<li><a href="C:\My Documents\webdesign\Games.HTML">Indoor games</a>
<li><a href="C:\My Documents\webdesign\Meditation.HTML">Meditation hall</a>
<li><a href="C:\My Documents\webdesign\Entertainment.HTML">Entertainment park
and greenaries.</a>
</Ol>
</BODY>
</HTML>
```

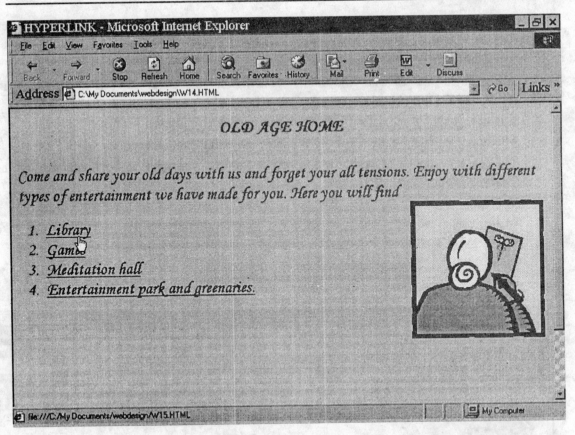

When the user clicks on the Library link the linked page opens. So before creating the link design all the web pages and then proceed. You can change the link color by the mentioning the color. Note that when you bring the cursor near the link the cursor changes to a hand sign.

Follow the code of Library linked page.

Code :

```
<HTML>
<HEAD>
<TITLE>Library</TITLE>
</HEAD>
<BODY Background="C:\Program Files\Common Files\Microsoft
Shared\Themes\citrus\cittext.gif">
<img align="left" width=200 height=200 src="C:\Program Files\Common Files\Microsoft
Shared\Clipart\cagcat50\Bs00554_.wmf">
<Center><Font size=15>Library</Center>
<hr color="Lime">
<Font size=4>
```

Here you will find books on all category History, Geography, Social Science, Economics, Arts & Culture, General Knowledge, Science etc.

Latest collection of Magazines will increase your knowledge.

Comic books like Chacha Chowdhury, Pinky, Batul the Great etc will make you smile like a child.

You can study at our Library from morning 7 am to 8 pm.

Afternoon from 1 am to 2 pm it remains close for lunch.

You can take books at your room too, but for that you have to be a member of the library.

To become a member you have to pay a membership fee of Rs 500/-.They can take any book in condition that they will return within 7 days.

</BODY>

</HTML>

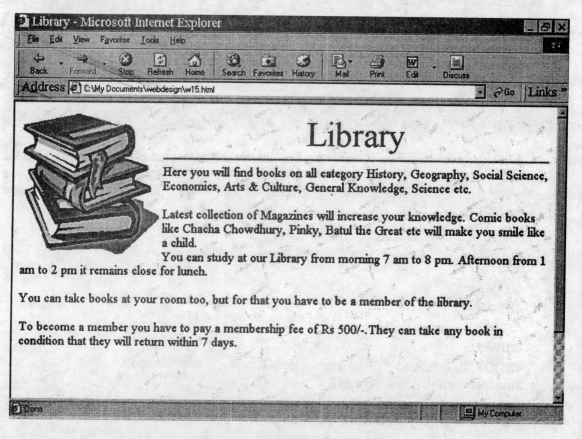

This page opens when the user clicks on the library link.

Follow the code of Games linked page.

Code :

```
<HTML>
<HEAD>
<TITLE>Games</TITLE>
</HEAD>
<BODY>
<center><H1>Enjoy Differnt types of games</H1>
<img height="330" src="C:\Program Files\Common Files\Microsoft
Shared\Clipart\cagcat50\Pe03738_.wmf"></center>
<P>
<B>Please Note</B><U>Select the games as per doctor's suggestions. </U></P>
</Body>
</Html>
```

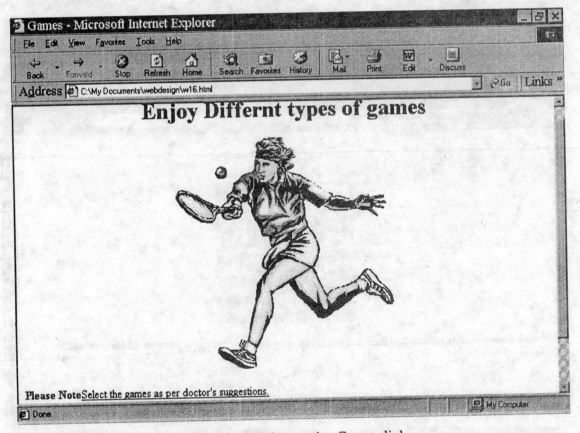

This page opens when the user clicks on the Games link.

Follow the code of Meditation linked page.

Code :

```
<HTML>
<HEAD>
<TITLE>meditation</TITLE>
</HEAD>
<BODY>
<center><H1>Prayer</H1>
<img src="C:\Program Files\Common Files\Microsoft
Shared\Clipart\cagcat50\Bd06455_.wmf"></center>
<P>
<B><I>Prayer starts from 6.30 p.m. to 7.30 p.m. It is not compulsory to attend the
prayer, but we advise to attend the prayer. </B></I></P>
</Body>
</Html>
```

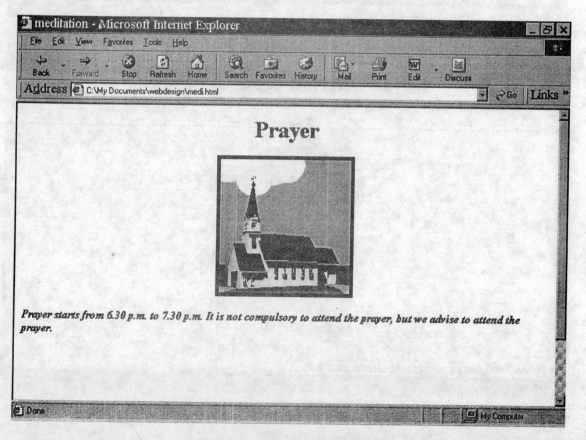

This page opens when the user clicks on the Meditation link.

Follow the code of Entertainment linked page.

Code :

```
<HTML>
<HEAD>
<TITLE>Entertainment Park</TITLE>
</HEAD>
<BODY>
<center><H1>Entertainment Park</H1><br><br>
<img src="C:\Program Files\Common Files\Microsoft
Shared\Clipart\cagcat50\Bd07270_.wmf"></center>
<font size=5>
<P>Our Entertainment park will provide you boating facility. The park looks beautifull
with different types of trees. In the mid of the park you will find a fountain which
shows water dance every evening.</P>
<P>The park welcomes you.</P>
</Body>
</Html>
```

Creating Link using images

Now lets create the link using images where images are used instead of text.

Follow the code, which shows the link on image.

Code :

```
<HTML>
<HEAD>
<TITLE>HYPERLINK</TITLE>
</HEAD>
<BODY Background="C:\Program Files\Common Files\Microsoft Shared\Stationery\Clear Day Bkgrd.jpg">
<h1><center>Greetings.Com</center></h1>
<Font size=4>
<p>Hi Users, this site is made especially for you to send greetings for your friends & relatives.</p><br><br>
<A href="C:\My Documents\webdesign\send.html" link="lime"><img width=100 height=100 src="C:\My Documents\webdesign\rose1.gif"></A>
<A href="C:\My Documents\webdesign\send1.html"><img width=100 height=100 src="C:\My Documents\webdesign\rose5.gif"></A>
<A href="C:\My Documents\webdesign\send2.html"><img width=100 height=100 src="C:\My Documents\webdesign\lili.gif"></A>
<A href="C:\My Documents\webdesign\send3.html"><img width=100 height=100 src="C:\My Documents\webdesign\rose.gif"></A>
<A href="C:\My Documents\webdesign\send4.html"><img width=100 height=100 src="C:\My Documents\webdesign\flower1.jpg"></A>
<A href="C:\My Documents\webdesign\send5.html"><img width=100 height=100 src="C:\My Documents\webdesign\flower3.jpg"></A>
<A href="C:\My Documents\webdesign\send6.html"><img width=100 height=100 src="C:\My Documents\webdesign\flower4.jpg"></A>
<br>
<br>
<Font style="Arial Black" size=6 color="yellow">
<marquee bgcolor="red">Click on the card to send it</marquee>
</BODY>
</HTML>
```

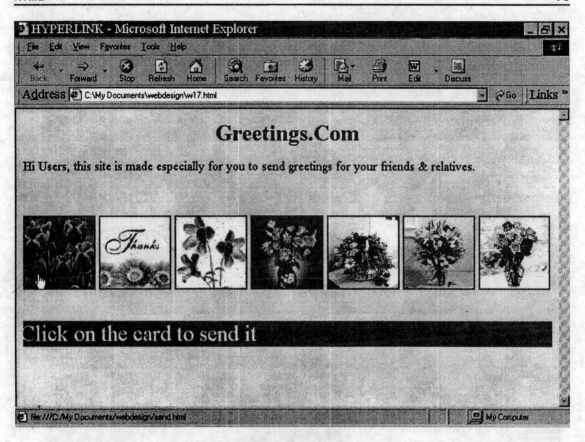

When the users click on any image it opens linked page.

Now follow the code of the linked page.

Code :

```
<HTML>
<HEAD>
<TITLE>Greetings.Com</TITLE>
</HEAD>
<BODY Background="C:\Program Files\Common Files\Microsoft Shared\Stationery\Clear
Day Bkgrd.jpg">
<h1><center>Greetings.Com</center></h1>
<center>
<img  width=150 height=150 src="C:\My Documents\webdesign\rose1.gif">
</center>
<br>
Enter your message<textarea name=t1 col=40 row=20>
</textarea>
<br>
```

```
Enter the e-mail address
<Input type="text" size=40><Br><Br>
<Input type="button" value="Send">
<Input type="button" value="Return"><Br><br>
<Font style="Arial Black" size=6 color="yellow">
<marquee bgcolor="red">
Thank You for visiting Greetings.Com
</marquee>
</BODY>
</HTML>
```

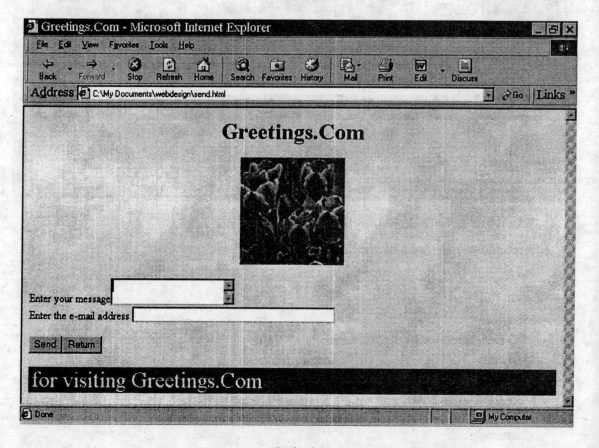

* * *

9

Frames

Frameset

Using Frameset we can set the web pages in the frame. This helps to divide the Browser window in row wise and in column wise. Imagine the whole window as 100% and then divide it according to the required percentage.

You have to begin with the <Frameset> tag and ends with </Frameset> tag.

For each Frame you have to mention the frame source. While creating frame if you set one part as 60 and for the other part you can mention it as * which will take the rest part i.e. the remaining 40%. Similarly while mentioning 50%, 50% you can also put *,* both are same.

Working with Frames

Follow the code, which breaks the window in two frames.

Code :

```
<Html>

<Head>

<Title>Quiz</Title>

</Head>

<Frameset cols="15%,85%">

<Frame src="C:\My Documents\webdesign\Frame.html">

<Frame src="C:\My Documents\webdesign\Frame2.html">

</Frameset>

</Html>
```

Code :

For Frame.html (i.e. 1st frame)

```
<Html>
<Head>
<Title>Frame</Title>
</Head>
<Body>
<img src="C:\My Documents\webdesign\gift6.jpg"><br>
<img src="C:\My Documents\webdesign\gift7.jpg"><br>
<img src="C:\My Documents\webdesign\gift9.jpg"><br>
<img src="C:\My Documents\webdesign\gift2.jpg"><br>
</Body>
</html>
```

Code :

For Frame2.html (i.e. 2nd frame)

```
<Html>
<Head>
<Title>Quiz</Title>
</Head>
<Body bgcolor="yellow" text="red">
<center><H2>Guess And Win</H2></center>
<font size=4>
<p>
Guess the price of these items and win fabulous prizes.</p>
<p>Just click on the correct price you think is correct and then click on the submit button.</p>
<p>Don't forget to give your e-mail address, because we will inform you by sending e-mail.</p>
<p>We wish you good luck</p>
<br>
No. 1 Item : <Input type="Radio" Name="r1"="on">Rs. 100
             <Input type="Radio" Name="r1"="on">Rs. 150
             <Input type="Radio" Name="r1"="on">Rs. 120
<br><br>
No. 2 Item : <Input type="Radio" Name="r2"="on">Rs. 200
             <Input type="Radio" Name="r2"="on">Rs. 250
             <Input type="Radio" Name="r2"="on">Rs. 240
<br><br>
```

No. 3 Item : <Input type="Radio" Name="r3"="on">Rs. 86
              <Input type="Radio" Name="r3"="on">Rs. 150
              <Input type="Radio" Name="r3"="on">Rs. 154

No. 4 Item : <Input type="Radio" Name="r4"="on">Rs. 90
              <Input type="Radio" Name="r4"="on">Rs. 160
              <Input type="Radio" Name="r4"="on">Rs. 128

Enter your e-mail address<Input type="e-mail" size=30>

<Input type="Submit" value="Submit">

</body>

</html>

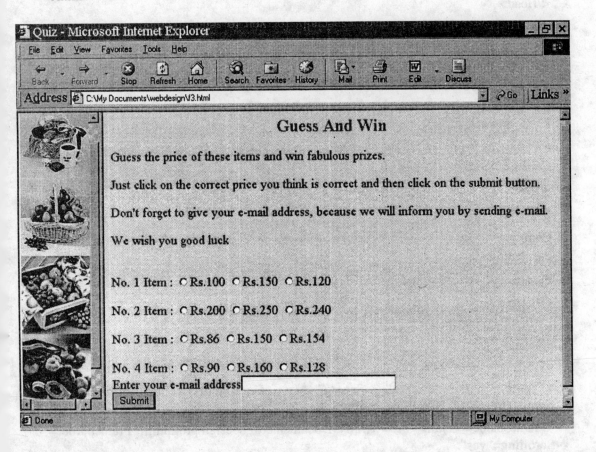

Creating target frames

We can create target frames, which makes your web more users friendly. In this example you will find the other features of the frame like border, scrolling property etc.

Using the Target frame you can call any web in a particular frame.

Follow the code, which shows the effect of target frames for ex. when the user clicks on the programming course the programming course details page appears in the right frame as it is targeted. Using this feature you can enhance the flexibility of browsing the web page for the users.

Code :

For Course Details page:

```
<Html>
<Head>
<Body>
<Title>Target</Title>
</Head>
<Body Bgcolor="lightgreen">
<Font size=5>
<B><U>Course Details</B></U><Br><Br>
<Font size=4>
<A href="C:\My Documents\webdesign\prof.html" target="details">Professional Course</A><Br><Br>
<A href="C:\My Documents\webdesign\prog.html" target="details">Programming Course</A><Br>
</Body>
</Html>
```

Code :

For Frame page

```
<Html>
<Head>
<Title>Target</Title>
</Head>
<Frameset cols="22%,*">
<Frame name="course" Src="C:\My Documents\webdesign\course.html" Frameborder="0" Scrolling="no">
<Frame name="details" Src="C:\My Documents\webdesign\prof.html" Frameborder="0" Scrolling="yes">
</Frameset>
</Html>
```

Code :

For Professional Course details page:

```
<Html>
<Head>
<Title>Target</Title>
</Head>
<Body Bgcolor="skyblue" text="red">
<Img align="left" height="400"
src="C:\WINDOWS\SYSTEM\OOBE\IMAGES\START.JPG">
<H1><center>Professional Course includes</H1>
<br><br>
<Font size=5>
Windows 98<br>
MS Word 2000<br>
MS Excel 2000<br>
MS Powerpoint 2000<br>
MS Access 2000<br>
Internet
</center>
<p>Course Duration-3 Months, 3 days a week(Mon,Wed & Fri) at 5.00 P.M.</p>
</Body>
</Html>
```

Code :

For Programming Course details page:

```
<Html>
<Head>
<Title>Target</Title>
</Head>
<Body Bgcolor="lightyellow" text="red">
<Img align="left" height="400"
src="C:\WINDOWS\SYSTEM\OOBE\IMAGES\START.JPG">
<H1><center>Programming Course includes</H1>
<br><br>
<Font size=5>
C++<br>
Visual Basic<br>
Visual Java<br>
Visual Foxpro<br>
Oracle<br>
Web Designing
</center>
<p>Course Duration-3 Months, 3 days a week(Tue, Thur & Sat) at 5.00 P.M.</p>
</Body>
</Html>
```

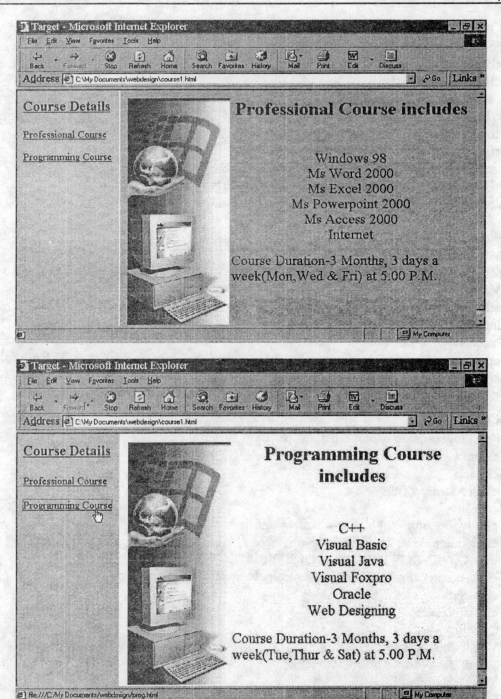

While dividing the frame the names of the frame is set as course and another as details. Now while creating the reference you have to give the target=details, so when the user clicks on that reference the page opens in the target frame i.e. in the details frame.

HTML PROJECT

Creating HTML pages is now easy for you. So lets create a project, which will bring more confidence in you.

This includes text, images, hyperlinks, tables, forms etc.

Home Page of the project

Code :

```
<Html>
<Head>
<Title>Computers Online</Title>
</Head>
<Body>
<Img align="right" height=100 width=100 src="C:\my documents\comp.jpg"><Br>
<Img height=100 width=350 src="C:\my documents\graphic1.jpg"><Br>
<Img align="right" height=200 width=200 src="C:\my documents\graphic2.jpg">
<Font size=4>
<P>We offer you the best Intel Pentium machine in a best price. Machines available of Different configurations, and if necessary you have the option to select your required configurations. A various range of Celeron,PII and PIII machines are avialable.</p>
<Table border=3>
<Tr>
<Th>Processor</Th><Th>Price</Th>
</Tr>
<Tr>
<Td><A Href="C:\My Documents\webdesign\Celeron400.html">Intel Celeron 400 multimedia</A></Td><Td>Rs.32990/-</Td>
</Tr>
<Tr>
<Td><A Href="C:\My Documents\webdesign\Celeron400.html">Pentium II 400 Mhz MM Kit</A></Td><Td>Rs.39800/-</Td>
</Tr>
<Tr>
<Td><A Href="C:\My Documents\webdesign\Celeron400.html">Celeron 400 Busybee </A></Td><Td>Rs.35490/-</Td>
</Tr>
<Tr>
<Td><A Href="C:\My Documents\webdesign\pIII.htm">Intel Pentium III 750</A> </Td><Td>Rs.35990/-</Td>
</Tr>
```

```
<Tr>
<Td><A Href="C:\My Documents\webdesign\pIII.htm">Intel Pentium III 933</A>
</Td><Td>Rs.36990/-</Td>
</Tr>
</Table><Br>
<hr color="Lime">
<I><H2><Center>We Accept</Center></H2></I>
<Center>
<A Href="C:\My Documents\webdesign\pay.htm">
<Img height="100" width="150"
src="C:\WINDOWS\SYSTEM\OOBE\IMAGES\bgvisa.jpg">
</A>
<A Href="C:\My Documents\webdesign\pay.htm">
<Img height="100" width="150"
src="C:\WINDOWS\SYSTEM\OOBE\IMAGES\bgmc.jpg">
</A>
<A Href="C:\My Documents\webdesign\pay.htm">
<Img height="100" width="150"
src="C:\WINDOWS\SYSTEM\OOBE\IMAGES\bgdiscov.jpg">
</A>
<A Href="C:\My Documents\webdesign\pay.htm">
<Img height="100" width="150"
src="C:\WINDOWS\SYSTEM\OOBE\IMAGES\bgjcb.jpg">
</A>
</Center>
<Center><H3>Company Offers</H3>
<A href="C:\My Documents\webdesign\comp.html">
<Img height=140 width=140
src="C:\WINDOWS\SYSTEM\OOBE\IMAGES\ball_ani.gif">
</A>
</Center>
<Marquee Bgcolor="Pink">
Online Computers offer a range of branded PCs with Exciting Gifts.
</Marquee>
</Body>
</Html>
```

Figure 1 of Computer Online web page

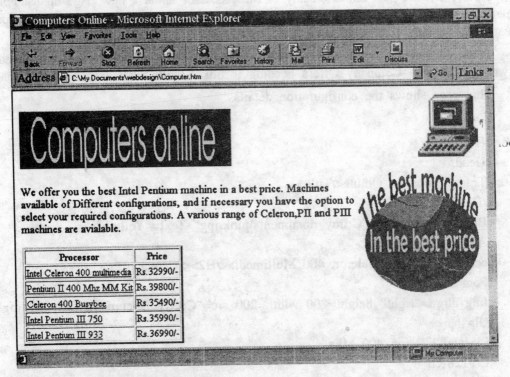

Figure 2 of Computer Online page

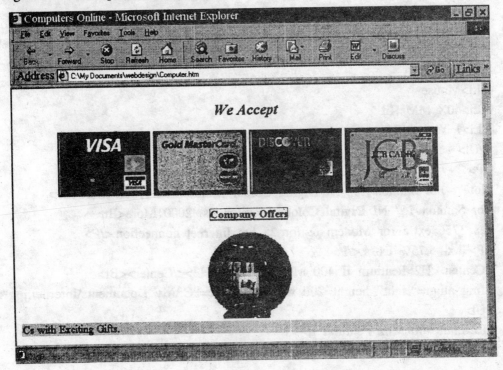

Now when the user clicks on any of the processor name a new page opens. For Intel Celeron 400 Multimedia, PII 400 Mhz MM Kit and Celeron 400 Busybee, another page is created mentioning their configurations details.

In the second portion of Computer.htm page the images of credit cards are linked with Pay.htm page. The Company Offers heading is linked with the Company Offers page.

This page shows the configuration details

Code :

```
<Html>
<Head>
<Title>Computers Online</Title>
</Head>
<Body Background="C:\my documents\pink.jpg" Text="Yellow">
<A Name="Top"></A>
<center><H2>Intel Celeron 400 Multimedia</H2></Center><Br>
<Font size=4>
<Img align="right" height=200 width=200 src="C:\My Documents\Graphic3.jpg">
<Ul>
<Li>Intel Celeron 400 Mhz
<Li>128KB
<Li>32 mb ram
<Li>6.4 GB HDD
<Li>1.44 FDD
<Li>104 Key Board
<Li>PCI VGA
<Li>Mouse
<Li>40X MM Kit
<Li>1 Year OSM
</Ul>
<P>
```

Note : For Samton 14" NI Digital Colour Monitor Rs. 1000 More
For Samton 15" NI Digital Colour Monitor Rs. 2000 More
Rs. 3756 extra for Modem & for 25 hrs Internet connection.</P>
<P>Tax- 5.75% extra.</P>
<Center><H2>Pentium II 400 Mhz MM Kit</H2></Center>
<Img align="right" height=200 width=200 src="C:\My Documents\Internet.jpg">
<Ul>
<Li>Intel 400 Mhz Pentium II
<Li>128KB

```
<Li>32 MB RAM
<Li>6.4 GB HDD
<Li>1.44 FDD
<Li>104 Key Board
<Li>AGP 4MB
<Li>Scrolling Mouse
<Li>48X MM Kit
<Li>14" Digital Colour Monitor
<Li>1 Year OSM
</Ul><Br>
```
Note. For Samton 15" NI Digital Colour Monitor Rs. 2000 More
Rs. 3756 extra for Modem & for 25 hrs Internet connection.
You can get the Encyclopedia CD just by paying Rs.300/-.
Tax- 5.75% extra.</P>
```
<Center><H2>Celeron 400 Busybee</H2></Center><Br>
<Img align="right" height=200 width=200 src="C:\My Documents\mouse.jpg">
<Ul>
<Li>Intel Celeron 400
<Li>128KB
<Li>32 MB RAM
<Li>4.3 GB HDD
<Li>1.44 FDD
<Li>104 Key Board
<Li>AGP 4MB
<Li>PCI Sound
<Li>Mouse
<Li>40X MM Kit
<Li>Win 98CD
<Li>1 Year OSM
</Ul>
```
Note. For Samton 15" NI Digital Colour Monitor Rs. 2000 More.
Rs. 3756 extra for Modem & for 25 hrs Internet connection.
Offering Printer worth Rs. 6900/- at Rs. 4000/-.
Tax- 5.75% extra.

```
<A Href="C:\My Documents\webdesign\Computer.htm">Home</A>
<A Href="#Top">Top</A></P>
</Body>
</Html>
```

Figure 1 (Configuration page)

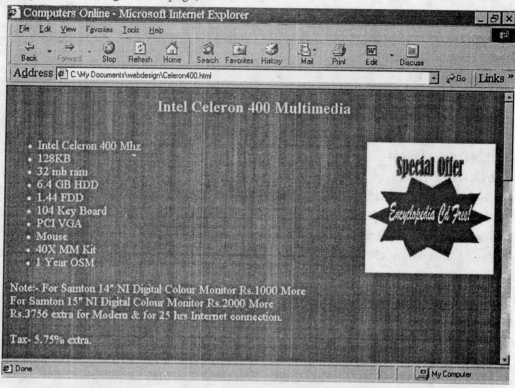

Figure – 2 (Configuration page)

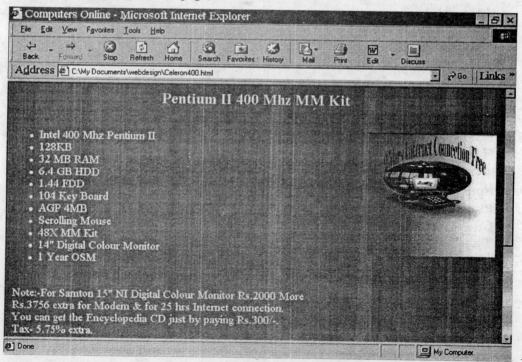

Figure 3 (Configuration page)

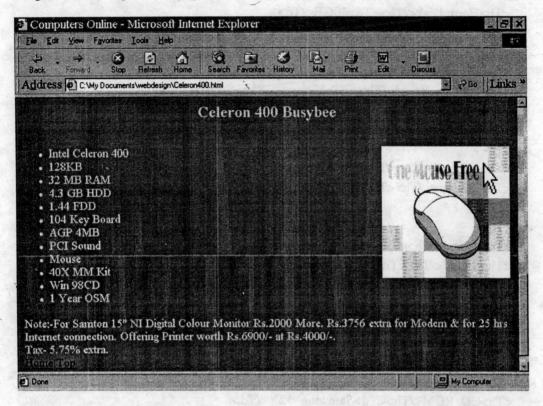

At the end of the page there are two links (1) Home, (2) Top. When the user clicks on Home it opens the Home page of the project i.e. Computer.htm, and while scrolling down the page when the user wants to scroll up at the top of the page, by clicking on Top, it takes the users at the top of the page.

The PIII.htm shows the details of the Pentium machines when the user clicks on Intel Pentium III 933 or on Intel Pentium III 750 on the Home page of the project.

Code : (Configuration details)

```
<Html>
<Head>
<Title>Computers Online</Title>
</Head>
<Body Background="C:\My Documents\sparkle.jpg" Text="Red">
<center><H2>Intel Pentium III</H2>
<Table border=4>
<Tr>
<Th>Processor</Th><Td>Intel Pentium III 933</Td>
<Th>Processor</Th><Td>Intel Pentium III 750</Td>
</Tr>
```

```
<Tr>
<Th>Hard Disk</Th><Td>40GB</Td>
<Th>Hard Disk</Th><Td>20GB</Td>
</Tr>
<Tr>
<Th>Mother Board</Th><Td>Mercurio 815 chipset</Td>
<Th>Mother Board</Th><Td>Mercurio 810E chipset</Td>
</Tr>
<Tr>
<Th>Memory</Th><Td>128 MB at 133 Mhz</Td>
<Th>Memory</Th><Td>64 MB at 133 Mhz</Td>
</Tr>
<Tr>
<Th>Sound</Th><Td>Sound Blaster</Td>
<Th>Sound</Th><Td>Integrated with motherboard</Td>
</Tr>
<Tr>
<Th>Modem</Th><Td>56K internal</Td>
<Th>Modem</Th><Td>Optional</Td>
</Tr>
<Tr>
<Th>CD ROM</Th><Td>Samsong 52X</Td>
<Th>CD ROM</Th><Td>Samsong 48X</Td>
</Tr>
<Tr>
<Th>Floppy Drive</Th><Td>Soni 1.44 MB</Td>
<Th>Floppy Drive</Th><Td>Soni 1.44 MB</Td>
</Tr>
<Tr>
<Th>Key Board</Th><Td>Samsong Multimedia</Td>
<Th>Key Board</Th><Td>104 Key Board</Td>
</Tr>
<Tr>
<Th>Monitor</Th><Td>15" Soni</Td>
<Th>Monitor</Th><Td>14" Soni</Td>
</Tr>
<Tr>
<Th>Mouse</Th><Td>Wheel Mouse</Td>
<Th>Mouse</Th><Td>3 Button Mouse</Td>
</Tr>
```

```
<Tr>
<Th>Case</Th><Td>Mini ATX</Td>
<Th>Case</Th><Td>Mini ATX</Td>
</Tr>
<Tr>
<Th>OS</Th><Td>Windows 2000</Td>
<Th>OS</Th><Td>Windows Me</Td>
HTML
</Tr>
<Tr>
<Th>Warranty</Th><Td>1 yr OSM</Td>
<Th>Warranty</Th><Td>1 yr OSM</Td>
</Tr>
</Table>
</Center>
</Body>
</Html>
```

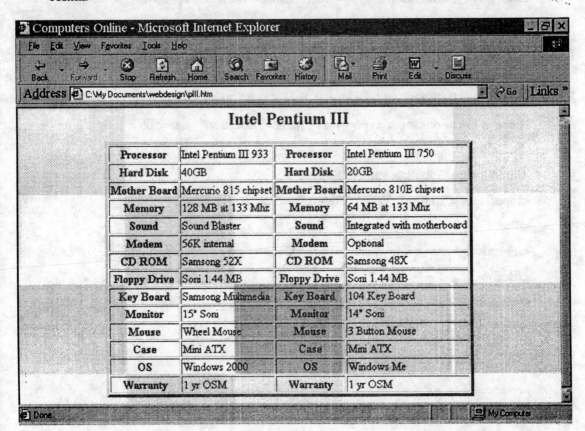

Intel Pentium III

Processor	Intel Pentium III 933	Processor	Intel Pentium III 750
Hard Disk	40GB	Hard Disk	20GB
Mother Board	Mercurio 815 chipset	Mother Board	Mercurio 810E chipset
Memory	128 MB at 133 Mhz	Memory	64 MB at 133 Mhz
Sound	Sound Blaster	Sound	Integrated with motherboard
Modem	56K internal	Modem	Optional
CD ROM	Samsong 52X	CD ROM	Samsong 48X
Floppy Drive	Soni 1.44 MB	Floppy Drive	Soni 1.44 MB
Key Board	Samsong Multimedia	Key Board	104 Key Board
Monitor	15" Soni	Monitor	14" Soni
Mouse	Wheel Mouse	Mouse	3 Button Mouse
Case	Mini ATX	Case	Mini ATX
OS	Windows 2000	OS	Windows Me
Warranty	1 yr OSM	Warranty	1 yr OSM

Code : (Payment details)

```
<Html>
<Head>
<Title>Form</Title>
</Head>
<Body Background="c:\my documents\leaf.jpg">
<Form>
<Center><H2>Fill the Payment Details</H2>
</Center>
<P>
<Font style="Niagara Solid">
<Font size=4>
Enter Your Card No. <Input type="text" name="Cardno" size=20><Br><Br>
Enter Your Name <Input type="text" name="Name" size=30>
<Br><Br>
Enter your Address<Input type="text" name="Address" size=50>
Pin: <Input type="text" name="Pin" size=10><Br><Br>
Enter your Delivery Address<Input type="text" name="Daddress" size=50><Br><Br>
Nearest Location<Input type="text" name="Location" size=50>
<Br><Br>
<Input type="Submit" Value="Submit">
<Input type="Button" Value="Return"></A>
</P>
</Form>
</Body>
</Html>
```

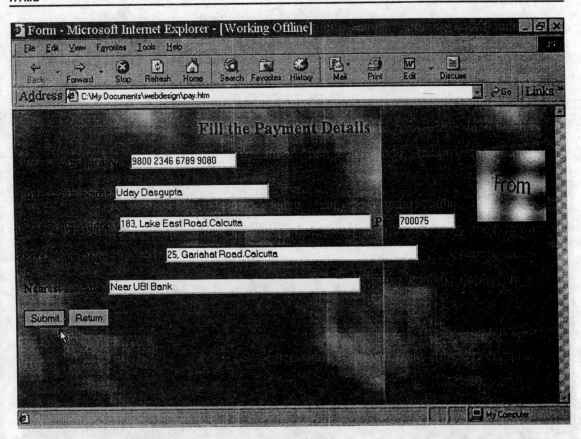

When the user clicks on movie of HPI offers it opens the Company offers page.

Code : (Company Offers)

```
<Html>
<Head>
<Title>Branded</Title>
</Head>
<Body Background="C:\my documents\compu.jpg">
<P>
<Font Size=7>
<Center><B></U>HPI Computer
Carnival</B></U></Center>
<Font size=5>
<P>
<Big>Intel Celeron 466</Big>/32MB SD RAM/6 GB HDD/1.44 MB FDD/HC Mouse/
4 MB AGP/Keyboard/40X Multimedia with Integrated sound/ Win 98/15" Samtron
Color Monitor/56 Kbps Internal Modem/Carnival CD Pack /
1 Yr OSM.<Br>
```

<Big>Intel P-III 450</Big>/32MB SD RAM/6 GB HDD/1.44 MB FDD/HC Mouse/4 MB AGP/Keyboard/40X Multimedia with Integrated sound/ Win 98/15" Samtron Color Monitor/56 Kbps Internal Modem/Carnival CD Pack/ Games CD/1 Yr OSM.

</P>

<Big>PC Bundle Offer</Big>/HCI CJ 1000 Printer + 75 Hrs Internet Connection + 56KBPS Modem.

</Body>

</Html>

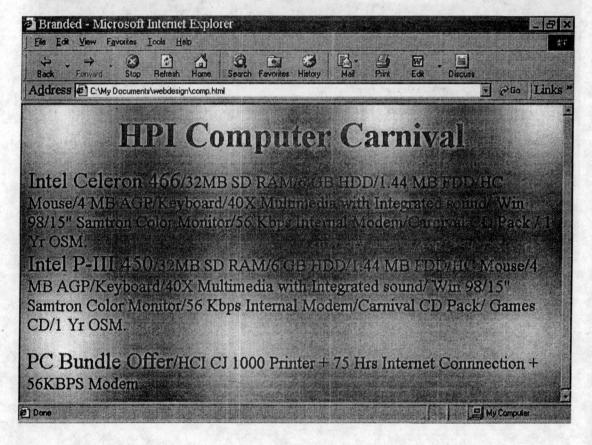

❋ ❋ ❋

DHTML

DHTML

10

Dynamic HTML

Now a day's user like to browse the web sites which are more attractive, dynamic and eye-catching. While creating a HTML page you had found some limitations but DHTML overcomes your limitations and fulfills your requirement.

DHTML allow the web authors to add interactive and dynamic features in the web, which makes the web more attractive. Do you think it's a new version of HTML? No. Do you think it's a new scripting language? No. DHTML will help you to break through your limitations.

The different advantages of DHTML

⇨ Creates interactive web pages

⇨ It removes the load of processing data, picture or may be an animation from the web server to the client machine.

⇨ It can be embedded in a HTML file without creating a separate file.

⇨ It's a combination of HTML, Scripting and object-oriented programming which creates beautiful web pages.

⇨ Dynamic HTML document displays on its own structure known as DOM (Document Object Model).

How does DOM works?

While working with HTML files you have seen HTML deals with the structure of the page. You can create paragraphs, headings, load picture, put background, create tables, frames etc. So you have displayed them as it appears. For ex. You have written a paragraph just by using the <P> tags and ended it with </P> tag. You haven't created a paragraph with different color, margin, indent etc. from other paragraphs. So this were the limitations you had with HTML, but now with DHTML you can create an own structure of the document with the help of DOM (Document Object Model).

You are embedding the styles in the same page (i.e. in the same text file) but DOM works in a different way. Here the browser identifies each element differently – where the element is placed, its attributes etc. In this way it can keep a track of each element of the browser (like headings, paragraphs, image etc). The browser makes a stack of similar objects after identifying them. For ex. You have put five headings so the browser creates a database and stores the record of the headings each time the pages gets uploaded.

Netscape is the first company to develop DOM since 1995 in Netscape Navigator 2.0. The developers were satisfied by its functionality. Later in Microsoft Internet Explorer DOM gets implemented.

At the beginning DOM was described as an Instance hierarchy of JavaScript object. Lets describe the both.

Instance

The object will not be created until and unless they appear on the web page. For ex. The link object will be empty in the absence of hyperlink.

Hierarchy

Each object created sets a relation with other objects. Follow the chain where you will find that the Browser sets relation with the window object and window object sets relation with document.

Again if you notice you will find that document has three objects links, anchors and form. The Form had a chain of form elements. So overall you can say that it maintains a descending hierarchy.

The object Hierarchy

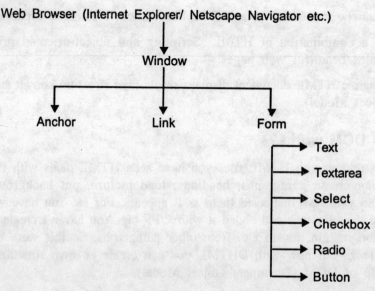

What is a Scripting Language?

A programming language required to control the different elements of the web page. For different appearance, to look at their settings, to create functions scripting language is used. The different scripting languages are JavaScript and VBScript. One thing you must remember i.e. the scripting language can run only in the browser, which is compatible with the scripting language like Netscape Navigator or Microsoft Internet Explorer.

Features of DHTML

Changing the tags. With the use of DOM you can change the tags and the matter of the style sheets.

Dynamic Fonts. Previously when you have worked with HTML fonts you have mentioned a font name and when you have viewed it in the browser it appears accordingly. But think of it when you are creating live projects, you are assigning a font which may not be available in the users machine. So you don't know how the font will appear after loading in the user machine.

To overcome this problem Netscape developed the idea of dynamic fonts. So with the font tag we are going to put a series of fonts according to the preference followed by a general type.

Positioning an Elements

When you have worked with HTML you couldn't position an element. Whereas with DHTML you can position an element according to your choice. If you are using Microsoft Internet Explorer it uses the style sheets <DIV> tags and if you are using Netscape Navigator you can use <DIV> tags and the <LAYER> tags.

Data Binding

You can use any database like SQL, ODBC and JDBC but you require an advance programming language for accessing a database. You can use any language as per your knowledge. Now a days Perl is used for Database handling which access the network and delivers required information.

(**Note.** It is not necessary to use Perl, you can use any other language.)

The World Wide Consortium (W3C)

The World Wide Consortium (W3C) is a recognized organization develops common standards. It also updates HTML and HTTP standards, mark-up Languages accessibility, related issues and browser implementations.

Microsoft and Netscape both were aware about the look of DHTML. Microsoft calls its implementation with capital 'D' and Netscape calls its implementation with lowercase 'd'.

The World Wide Consortium (W3C) has developed its own recommendations for DHTML. The different capabilities are listed below.

The Key components of the W3C DOM are universal. So that the user can use it in any browser and on any computer i.e. there is no limitations on computer configuration also.

DOM should be language independent. W3C wanted to separate DOM from different languages. The properties of the DOM can be used on any language without changing its structure.

DOM is accessible for all users. A graphical browser can work with text, images and all other visual manipulations ranging from heading styles, tables etc.

There are some non-graphical browsers like lynx. Different browsers have some limitations too. For ex. Netscape.

W3C maintains the standard that promote HTML and DOM accessibility for people.

The last requirement is security, privacy and validity. Discussion rise between the groups who are working on this recommendation matter. There is a controversy in this regard. One says the page can be modified and other part says it may lead some problem where it relates to user agent and history list.

DOM Capabilities

Navigation Structure. This refers regarding navigation between the documents. Finding a parent element or a child element.

Manipulation of Content. This refers to manipulate the content and document. At any portion you can change the script or the content. For ex. You can change H1 to H2, you may change the color etc.

Event Model. Event model makes the page interactive. This includes a wide variety of possible activities like mouse movements, mouse clicks, key press etc.

✳ ✳ ✳

11

Style Sheets

Style Sheet is used to control the formatting of HTML tags. Generally formatting HTML tags had some limitations. But Style Sheets opens a gateway for the web designers to create design and format according to their choice.

Cascading Style Sheets (CSS)

The browser follows an order – called a cascade – to interpret the information. Using CSS you can put multiple styles in a HTML document.

Using Cascading Style Sheets (CSS) you can create styles for your web page. The different features of styles sheets are added in the HTML document for better appearance of the page and it doesn't affect the HTML document. Using style sheets you can improve various features like fonts, size, weight, margins, indent, paragraphs, background, graphics etc.

The different Style Sheets are

Inline Style Sheets. It adds a specific style to the document controlled by the tags. For ex. You want to color a paragraph with red. Then mention it as red and control the paragraph settings inside the span tags.

Embedded Style Sheets. This method embeds the styles inside the <Style> tags and ends with </Style> tags. They are placed inside the <Body> tags and inside

External (Linked) Style Sheets. This method embeds the style from an external file. For ex. Style is created and saved with an extension .css. Later it is linked with the HTML document.

Working with Inline Style

Here you have to set the style with the tags. Suppose you want to set the font style of the paragraph you should write <P style = "font style: Italic">

Follow the code, which shows Inline style

Code :

```
<Html>
<Head>
<Title>Inline</Title>
</Head>
<Body bgcolor="lime">
<center><H1 Style="background-color:blue" id="h1">Inline Style</H1></Center>
<P Style="font-size:14pt" "font-weight:bold" "font-style:italic" id="p1">
This is a type of style setting. Here the fonts size of the paragraph is 14pt.
The font appears bold and the font style appears in italic.</P>
<P>
The different types of styles are <Br>
<Span Style="font-weight:bold" id="s1">
Inline Style<Br>
Embeded Style<Br>
Linked Style<Br>
</Span>
</P>
<P style="font-size=16pt" "Color:yellow" id="p2"> This example describes the inline
style</P>
</Body>
</Html>
```

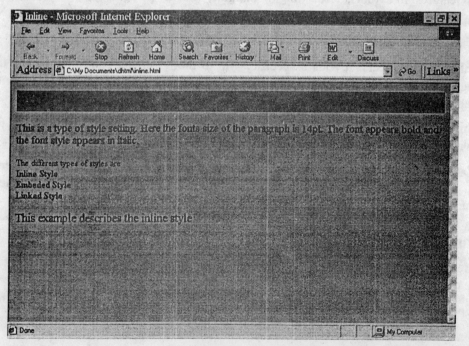

Working with Embedded Style

Here you have to set the style inside the <Style> tags. First create the HTML document. Then embed the style in the <Style> tags in the editor. Remember if you have set the style for H2 and while creating the HTML document you are not using the H2 then it is of no use. Create the HTML document with the tags for which you had set the styles.

Follow the code, which shows Embedded Style

Code :

```
<Html>
<Head>
<Title>Embedded</Title>
</Head>
<STYLE>
BODY {background-color:lightblue; color:red; margin - left:0.5in; margin - right:0.5in}
H1 {background-color:yellow; color:red}
H2 {color:blue}
P {font-size:14pt; color:green;}
</STYLE>
</Head>
<Body>
<Br><Br>
<H1><center>Vision 2000</H1>
<H2>Computer Education</H2></Center>
<P>Authorised software user of Microsoft. We are providing education of various Microsoft Software.
We are having ATC from FACT. Other than that we teach different subjects like
DTP i.e Desktop Publishing. Further we have 3yrs Diploma course, E-commerce course etc. </P>
</Body>
</Html>
```

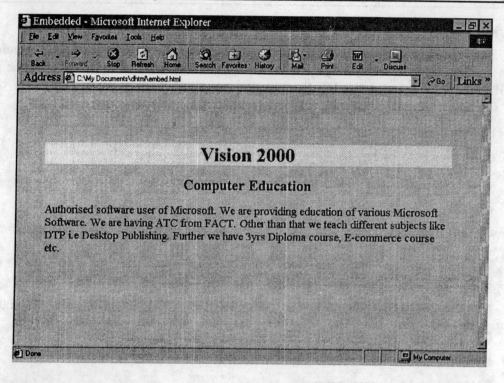

Working with Link Style

Link style sheets are quite helpful. You can link it to any files according to your choice. Still now you have seen that you have to create the style each time you create a page. But with Link style you can create the style in a different file and then just link it with the HTML document.

What you have to do? Open the editor for ex. Notepad. Then start from the <Style> tag instead of <HTML> tag. Now set the styles for each element as you have done in the previous example. Later when you finish save it with an extension of .css. For ex. Style1.css.

Next part is to create a HTML document separately and then set the link to this file. For ex. <link rel=stylesheet href= "Style1.css" type= "text/css">

In the same way you could have linked a JavaScript Style sheets too. Then the type would change to text/js.

For ex.

<STYLE>
BODY {background-color:lightblue; color:red; margin - left:0.5in; margin - right:0.5in}
H1 {background-color:yellow; color:red}
H2 {color:blue}
P {font-size:14pt; color:green;}
</STYLE>

This style is created and saved in a file named as Style1.css.

Creating the link

```
<HTML>
<Head>
<Title>Link</Title>
<link rel=stylesheet href= "Style1.css" type= "text/css">
</Head>
</HTML>
```

And the output will be same as embedded style sheet. It will set the style tags from the link file and change the HTML document.

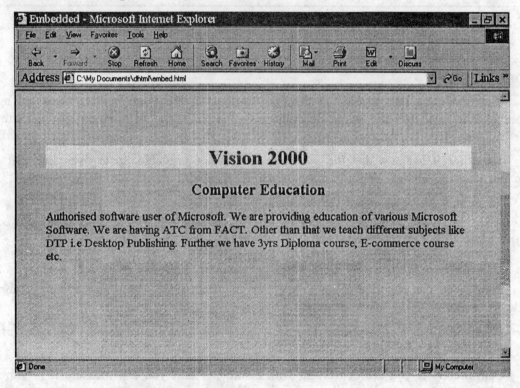

Planning for creating a Web page

Before we create a web page we need to chalk out the plan.

First get the answer for the following questions

What is the purpose?

For whom you are creating?

What are the elements you require?

What are the necessary items you need to highlight?

Once you collect the answers of these questions its easy for you to create the web page. So remember these points while creating a web page.

✷ ✷ ✷

12

Font Attributes

Font Family

The first thing that appears in the Font attribute is the Font Family. There are many types of font available and while describing a style you have to mention the font family. For ex. (Font-Family: Arial)

Sometime it happens that the particular font is not available, so to overcome that you can put choices. For ex. (Font-Family: Arial, Arial Black)

So in this way you make the selection of font family.

Font size

Five types of units of measurement are available to set the size of the font.

Point. You can describe it in points. For ex. (Font-size: 18pt). This is very common and you will find it in many examples.

Pixels. You can measure fonts in pixels too. Pixels is common for the computer users. Ex. (Font-size: 18 px).

Centimeter. If you are conversant with centimeter unit you can measure it in cm. Ex. (Font-size: 6 cm).

Inches. You can measure it in inches. (Font-size: 1 in).

Percentage. This is the last type where you can set the percentage to set the font size. For ex.(Font-size: 180 %).

Font style

Style attribute helps you to set the style of the font. For ex. (Font-style: Italic). To set the default status of the font set the attribute to font-style: normal. Another Font-style attribute is oblique which is quite similar to italic.

Font weight. Weight represents the thickness of the font. You can set it to extra light, demi-light, light, medium, extra-bold, demi-bold and bold. Before you assign the font-weight be sure it is available because except bold other Font-weights may vary in different platforms.

Text-decoration. The Text-decoration attributes are none, underline, italic and line-through. For ex. (Text-decoration: Underline)

Line-height. It set the line spacing between the lines of text.

For ex. P (line-height: 12 pt)

Working with Font Attributes

Follow this ex. Where you will find all the font attributes.

Code :

```
<Html>
<Head>
<Title>Text Formatting</Title>
</Head>
<Style>
H1 {font-family:Lucida Handwriting; font-size:20; font-weight: bold; text-decoration: underline}

P {font-family:News Gothic MT; Font-size:14pt; font-style: Italic;
 line-height: 20 pt}
</Style>
<Body>
<Center><H1>World Champ</H1></Center>
<P>
Computer World is going to organise a summer camp. Children's ageing 10-15 yrs can join the camp. Candidates have to register their details by 25th February 2001. To register they have to bring their Id card and two passport size photographs. <P>
</Body>
</Html>
```

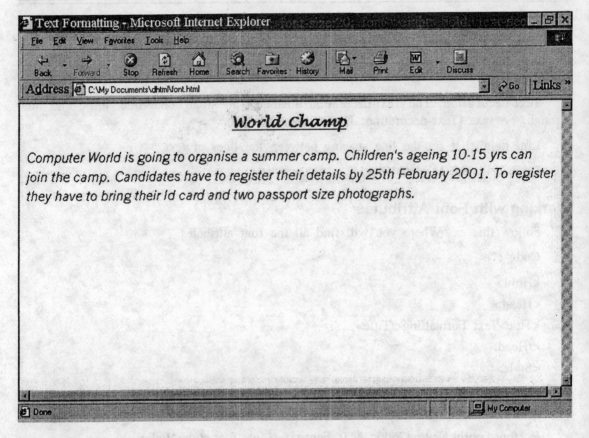

Working with Margin

While working with HTML you might have faced problem for placing the text, but with DHTML you can set the margins of the text for better performance. All the measurement units are similar, as you have seen in font-size.

Margin-left. Sets the left margin of the text. For ex. Margin-left: 1 in.

Margin-right. Sets the right margin of the text. For ex. Margin-right: 1 in.

Margin-top. Sets the top margin of the text. For ex. Margin-top: 1.5 in.

Follow the code, which sets the text margin

Code :

```
<Html>
<Head>
<Title>Text Formatting</Title>
</Head>
<Style>
Body {margin-left: 1 in; margin-right: 1 in; margin-top: 0.10 in}
H1 {font-family:Lucida Handwriting; font-size:20; font-weight: bold; text-decoration:
underline}
```

P {font-family:News Gothic MT; Font-size:14pt; font-style: Italic; line-height: 20 pt}
</Style>
<Body>
<Center><H1>World Champ</H1></Center>
<P>
Computer World is going to organise a summer camp. Children's ageing 10-15 yrs can join the camp. Candidates have to register their details by 25th February 2001. To register they have to bring their Id card and two passport size photographs. <P>
</Body>
</Html>

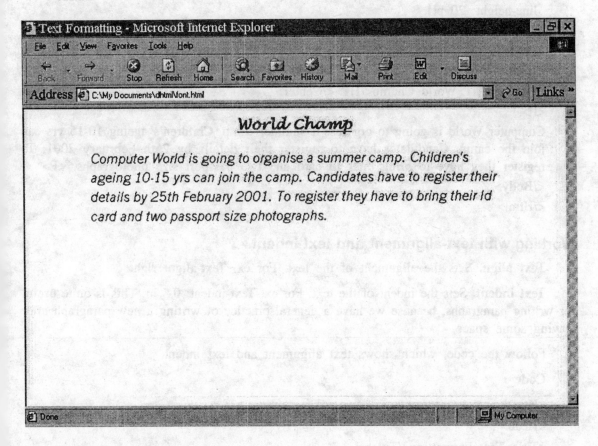

Working with comment tags.

When the browser is incompatible it displays the page in a text format so to hide the styles from incompatible browser write the styles inside the comment tags. The browser, which is style-incompatible, ignores the comment and displays the page.

Follow the style code, which is written inside the comment tags.

```
<Html>
<Head>
<Title>Text Formatting</Title>
</Head>
<Style>
<! —
Body {margin-left: 1 in; margin-right: 1 in; margin-top: 0.10 in}
H1 {font-family:Lucida Handwriting; font-size:20; font-weight: bold; text-decoration:
underline}
P {font-family:News Gothic MT; Font-size:14pt; font-style: Italic;
  line-height: 20 pt}
—>
</Style>
<Body>
<Center><H1>World Champ</H1></Center>
<P>
```

Computer World is going to organise a summer camp. Children's ageing 10-15 yrs can join the camp. Candidates have to register their details by 25th February 2001. To register they have to bring their Id card and two passport size photographs. <P>

```
</Body>
</Html>
```

Working with text-alignment and text-indent.

Text align. Sets the alignment of the text. For ex. Text-align: right.

Text indent. Sets the indent of the text. For ex. Text-indent: 0.5 in. This is quite useful for writing paragraphs, because we have a general practice of writing a new paragraph after leaving some space.

Follow the code, which shows text alignment and text indent.

Code :

```
<Html>
<Head>
<Title>Text Formatting</Title>
</Head>
<Style>
Body {margin-left: 1 in; margin-right: 1 in; margin-top: 0.10 in}
H1 {font-family:Lucida Handwriting; font-size: 20; font-weight: bold; text-decoration:
underline}
```

H2 {font-family:Arial Black; font-size: 18; font-weight:semi-bold; text-align: right}

P {font-family:News Gothic MT; Font-size:14pt; font-style: Italic; line-height: 20 pt; text-indent: 0.5 in}

</Style>

<Body>

<Center><H1>World Champ</H1></Center>

<P>

Computer World is going to organise a summer camp. Children's ageing 10-15 yrs can join the camp. Candidates have to register their details by 25th February 2001. To register they have to bring their Id card and two passport size photographs. <P>

<H2>Rules.</H2>

<P>The candidates should attend the camp at 7 pm. They are not allowed to carry food packets. Food will be provided by us. They should come in uniform, other dresses are not allowed.</P>

</Body>

</Html>

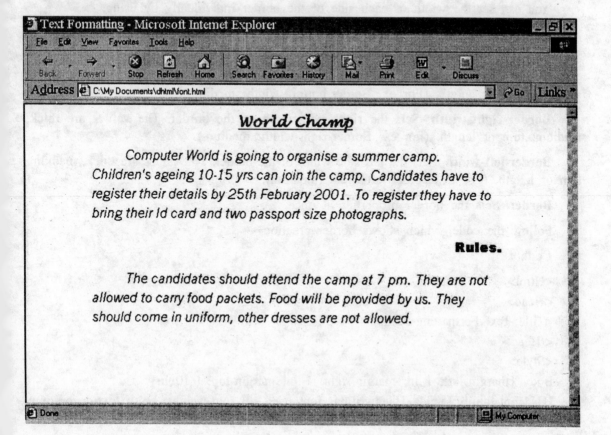

Working with borders

To make the text more attractive you can put borders. The different border attributes are mention below:

Border Attributes

Border-style. Sets the border style. (For ex. Border-style: Solid). The different types of styles are Solid, groove, double, ridge, inset, outset.

Border-color. Sets the border color. You can write the color name or the color code (For ex. Border-color: blue).

Border-width. Sets the border width. The values are thick, medium, thin or length. (For ex. Border-width: medium)

Border-top. Sets the width, color, and style of the top of the border.

Border-bottom. Sets the width, color, and style of the bottom of the border.

Border-right. Sets the width, color, and style of the right side of the border.

Border-left. Sets the width, color, and style of the left side of the border.

You can set the width of each side of the border individually by using,

Border-top-width. Sets the top width of the border. The values are thick, medium, thin or length. (For ex. Border-top-width: medium).

Border-bottom-width. Sets the bottom width of the border. The values are thick, medium, thin or length. (For ex. Border-bottom-width: medium).

Border-right-width. Sets the right side width of the border. The values are thick, medium, thin or length. (For ex. Border-right-width: medium).

Border-left-width. Sets the left side width of the border. The values are thick, medium, thin or length. (For ex. Border-left-width: medium).

Border. Sets the border properties at once.

Follow the code, which shows border creation

Code :

```
<Html>
<Head>
<Title>Text Formatting</Title>
</Head>
<Style>
Body {margin-left: 1 in; margin-right: 1 in; margin-top: 0.10 in}
H1 {font-family:Lucida Handwriting; font-size: 20; font-weight: bold; text-decoration: underline}
```

H2 {font-family:Arial Black; font-size: 18; font-weight:semi-bold; text-align: right}

P {font-family:News Gothic MT; Font-size:14pt; font-style: Italic;line-height: 20 pt; text-indent: 0.5 in; border-style: outset; border-top-width: thick; border-bottom-width: thin}

</Style>

<Body>

<Center><H1>World Champ</H1></Center>

<P>

Computer World is going to organise a summer camp. Children's ageing 10-15 yrs can join the camp. Candidates have to register their details by 25th February 2001. To register they have to bring their Id card and two passport size photographs. </P>

<H2>Rules.</H2>

<P>The candidates should attend the camp at 7 pm. They are not allowed to carry food packets.

Food will be provided by us. They should come in uniform, other dresses are not allowed.</P>

</Body>

</Html>

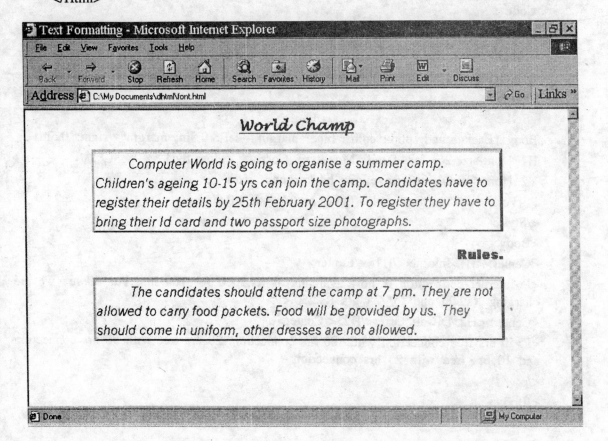

13

Working with Background and Colours

You can set background color on different web elements. You can set a background color for the body of the web and again you can set background color for a heading also. Background color makes the web attractive.

Follow the code, which shows the background color effect

Code :

```
<Html>
<Head>
<Title>Text Formatting</Title>
</Head>
<Style>
Body {Background: pink; color: blue; margin - left: 0.5in; margin - right: 0.5in}
H1 {font-size:26; font-family:Monotype Corsiva; color: red}
H2 {font-size:24; color: yellow; background: red}
P {Font-size:18pt; font style: Italic; text - indent:0.5in}
</Style>
<Body>
<Center><H1>Internet</H1></Center>
<P>Internet connection is now available at Rs.1000 for 100 hrs. For 50 hrs we are
charging Rs.500 and for 25 hrs Rs.250.<P>
<Center><H2>Diwali Offer</H2></Center>
<P>50 hrs free connection with 100 hrs connection. 20 hrs free with 50 hrs connection
and 10 hrs free with 25 hrs connection.
</p>
</Body>
</Html>
```

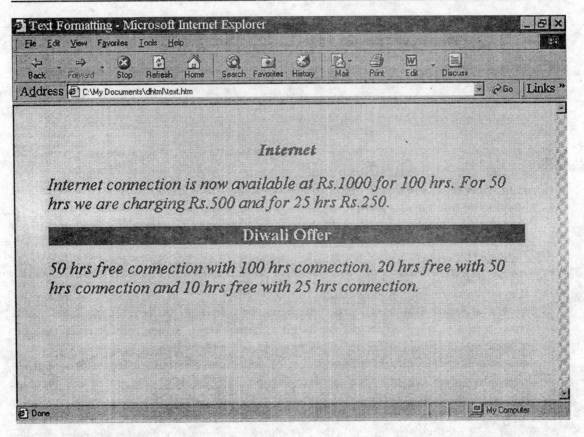

Creating a Group

Grouping style sheets assigns the same attributes for each element, which are assigned in the group tags. Say for ex. You are going to create H2, H3, H4, which will have the same attributes, so instead of mentioning each of them, we can create a group to mention all the attributes at a time. So instead of writing

H2 {font-family: Arial Black; font-size: 15 pt; font-style: oblique; color: yellow; background: green}

Then

H3 {font-family: Arial Black; font-size: 15 pt; font-style: oblique; color: yellow; background: green}

Again

H4 {font-family: Arial Black; font-size: 15 pt; font-style: oblique; color: yellow; background: green}

We will write in a group

H2, H3, H4 {font-family: Arial Black; font-size: 15 pt; font-style: oblique; color: yellow; background: green}

Now follow the example where you will find the group attributes and body attributes, which you have learned previously.

Code :

```
<Html>
<Head>
<Title>Group</Title>
</Head>
<Style>
H2, H3, H4 {font-family: Arial Black; font-size: 15 pt; font-style: oblique;
color: yellow; background: green}
Body {font-family: san-serif; font-size: 12 pt; line-height: 14 pt; font-
weight: bold; font-style: italic; font-align: justify; color: red; margin-left: 0.30 in; margin-
right: 0.30 in; margin-top: 0.40 in}
</Style>
<Body Bgcolor= "yellow">
<Center><H2>Garments Sale</H2></Center><Br>
We are giving a sale on all types of garments. You will get here suits, shirts, pants,
jeans, cotton pants, leather jackets, T-shirts, casual wear, sarees, salwar suits etc.<Br>
<Center><H3>Special offer for Children</H3></Center><Br>
For childrens you will get a huge range of collection of frocks, pants, shirts, T-shirts,
Baba-suit, gallies, ghagra, churidars etc. We are offering 10% discount if the purchase
price is more than Rs.500.
<Center><H4>Winter Special</H4></Center><Br>
Under one roof we are giving sale for winter garments too. Shawls, sweater, woolen
jackets, blankets are available.
</Body>
</Html>
```

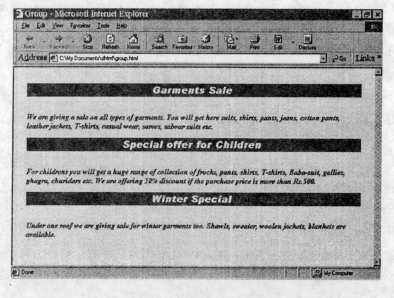

Working with Span tag

Span tag begins with <span> and ends with </span>. Using it you can set the styling rules and embed it in any portion of the text.

Follow the example where you will find the first letter of the paragraph is changed using the span tag.

Code :

```
<Html>
<Head>
<Title>Span</Title>
</Head>
<Style>
H2, H3, H4 {font-family: Arial Black; font-size: 14 pt; font-style: oblique; color: yellow; background: green}
Body {margin-left: 0.30 in; margin-right: 0.30 in; margin-top: 0.40 in}
p {font-family: Verdana; font-size: 12 pt; font-style: normal; font-weight: bold; color: blue}
</Style>
<Body Bgcolor= "yellow">
<Center><H2>Garments Sale</H2></Center>
<P><Span style="font-family: magneto; font-size: 20 pt; color: red; font-weight: bold">W</Span>e are giving a sale on all types of garments. You will get here suits, shirts, pants, jeans, cotton pants, leather jackets, T-shirts, casual wear, sarees, salwar suits etc.</P>
<Center><H3>Special offer for Children</H3></Center>
<P><Span style="font-family: magneto; font-size: 20 pt; color: red; font-weight: bold">F</Span>or childrens you will get a huge range of collection of frocks, pants, shirts, T-shirts, Baba-suit, gallies, ghagra, churidars etc. We are offering 10% discount if the purchase price is more than Rs.500.</P>
<Center><H4>Winter Special</H4></Center>
<P><Span style="font-family: magneto; font-size: 20 pt; color: red; font-weight: bold">U</Span>nder one roof we are giving sale for winter garments too. Shawls, sweater, woolen jackets, blankets are available.</P>
</Body>
</Html>
```

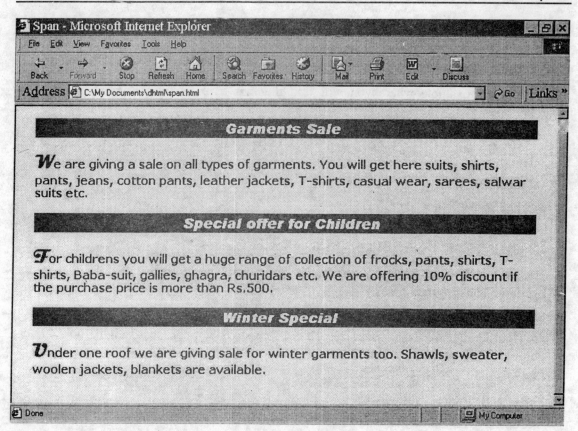

✳ ✳ ✳

14

Working with List Attributes

Various types of list styles are available like Disc, circle, square, decimal, upper-roman, lower-roman, upper-alpha, lower-alpha, none.

Follow the code, which displays a list

Code :

```
<Html>
<Head>
<Title>List</Title>
</Head>
<Style>
H1 {font-family: Monotype Corsive; font-size: 18 pt; font-weight: bold; text-decoration:
underline; color: red}
Body {margin-left: 0.30 in; margin-right: 0.30 in}
p {font-family: Verdana; font-size: 12 pt; font-style: normal; font-weight: bold; color:
blue}
UL {list-style-type: lower-alpha; font-family: Verdana; font-size: 16; font-weight:
bold;color: red}
</Style>
<Body Bgcolor= "yellow">
<Center><H1>Syllabus for 1st semister</H1></Center>
<P>
Dear Students</P>
<P>We wish you all the best for your 1st semister exam. We are giving you the
syllabus details and we going to declare the exam date on 25<sup>th</sup>November
2001.</P>
<P>Syllabus details:</P>
```

```
<Ul>
<Li>Windows 98
<Li>Ms Office 2000
<Li>Internet
<Li>C++
<Li>Visual Basic
<Li>Java
<Li>HTML
<Li>DHTML
<Li>Java Script
</Ul>
</Body>
</Html>
```

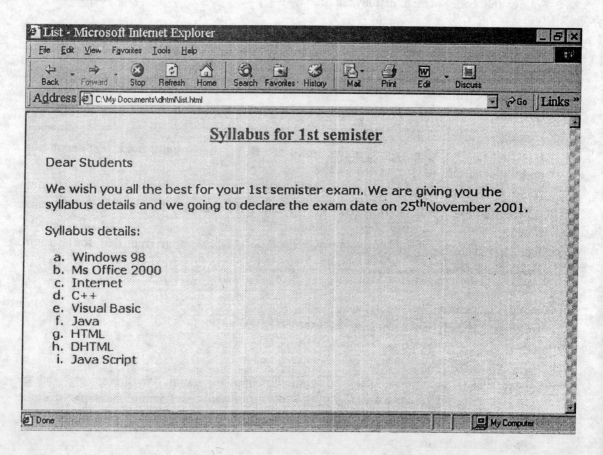

Assigning Classes

When you need variations in a style you can assign class by adding an extension name on HTML tags. You can add any name according to your choice. For ex. You require adding H1 two times but in two different formats then you can use class. You can apply class directly or in a part using the <Span> tags.

Follow the example where you will find one paragraph has been created by using class.

Code :

```
<Html>
<Head>
<Title>Class</Title>
</Head>
<Style>
H2 {Font-family: Lucida Console; Font-size: 22}
P {Font-family: Lucida Sans Unicode; Font-size: 16; color: green; text-align: justify}
.Information {Font-family: Impact; Font-style: Italic; Font-size: 16;Line-height:16 pt;
color:brown; text-align: justify}
</Style>
</Head>
<Body>
<Center><H2>DHTML</H2>
<P>Using DHTML we can make our HTML pages more dynamic. We can add style
for headings, body, paragraphs etc. The different font-attributes are font-family, font-
size, font-style, font-weight etc. We can add background colors, font colors. We can
set the margin, indent and alignment of the text. </P>
<P class="information"> Another important feature is class which allows to bring
variation in styles. Say you want to differentiate a paragraph from other paragraphs,
which is more important, and you want to highlight it by changing its style. Class will
help you to do this work. We can assign a class by mentioning a name. And later we
can call that class by its name.</P>
</Body>
</Html>
```

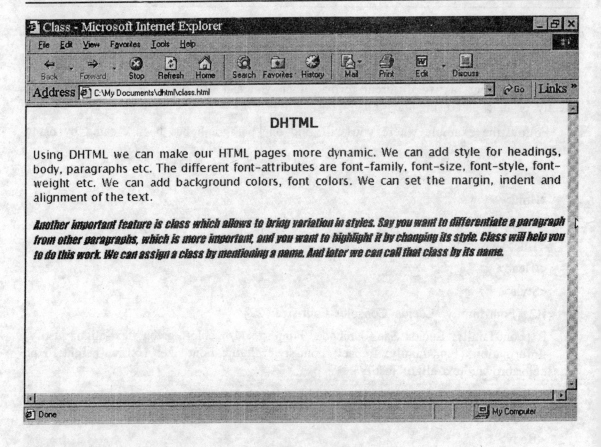

Working with Class using the <Span> tags

Using the <Span> tags you can set a boundary for the class.

Follow the code where <Span> tags are used to set the boundary for a class

Code :

```
<Html>
<Head>
<Title>Class</Title>
</Head>
<Style>
H1 {Font-size: 14 pt; Font-weight: bold; Font-style: normal}
P {Font-size: 12 pt; Font-weight: bold; Font-style: Italic; Color: red}
.Topic{Font-Family: Imprint Mt Shadow, Mordern No. 20; Font-size: 13 pt; Font-weight: bold; Font-style: Italic; Color: blue}
UL {List-style-type:square; Font-size: 12; Font-weight: bold}
</Style>
```

```
<Body Bgcolor="Tan">
<H1><Center>Book Shop</Center></H1>
<P>In our shop you will find a range of computer books. Beside that we are having
tutorial Cds, Games Cds, Floppy, and stationery. Follow the list for detail information.</
P>
<P><Span class="Topic">Application</Span> Books</P>
<Ul>
<Li>Ms Office 2000
<Li>Page Maker 6.5
<Li>Corel Draw 9.0
<Li>Photoshop 5.5
</Ul>
<P><Span class="Topic">Programming</Span> Books</P>
<Ul>
<Li>C++
<Li>Visual Basic 6.0
<Li>Foxpro 2.6
<Li>Visual Java
</Ul>
</Body>
</Html>
```

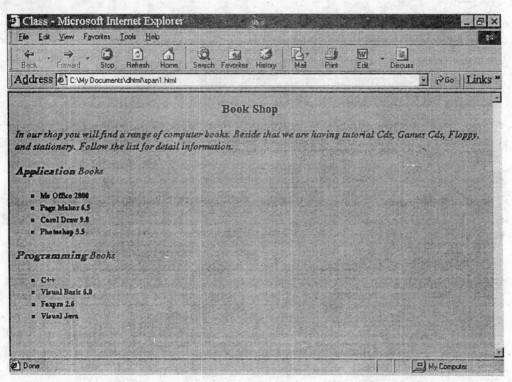

PROJECT ON DHTML

Now workout the project, which cover all above discussed topics. First create the page then create the link. You can put text according to your choice.

This is the introduction page. A link is set with the news.html page.

Code :

```
<HTML>
<Head>
<Title>News World</Title>
</Head>
<Style>
Body {background-color: green; color:yellow; margin-left:0.5in; margin-right:0.5in; text-align:justify}
H1{Font-family:Arial Black, Arial; font-size=18pt; font-weight:bold; background-color:red; color:white}
H2{Font-family:Arial Black, Arial; font-size=17pt; font-weight:bold; Text-align:right; background-color:red}
P{Font-family:Lucida Fax,Lucida Handwriting,Lucida Sans; font-size:16; font-style:Italic}
</Style>
<Body>
<H1>News World</H1>
<P>We deliver you the latest news of the world at a single click!. We give you information on Government Sector, Public relations, Entertainment,
Employment, Matrimonial etc. <P>
<P>On Monday you will find our Kids World paper. This paper gives all the detail information of the schools and Institution who is taking necessary actions in development of tender minds.
<P>
<P>On Tuesday you will get our Female World paper. This paper contains many items like Development done by female. It also contains required information like parlour, Health center, Shopping, Cooking etc.</P>
<P>
On Wednesday we cover Employment news. On Thursday we will find the matrimonial detail. Sunday we have the special coverage on Public Relations.</P>
<A Href="C:\My Documents\dhtml\news.html"><H2>Click Here to Join In.</H2></A>
</Body>
</HTML>
```

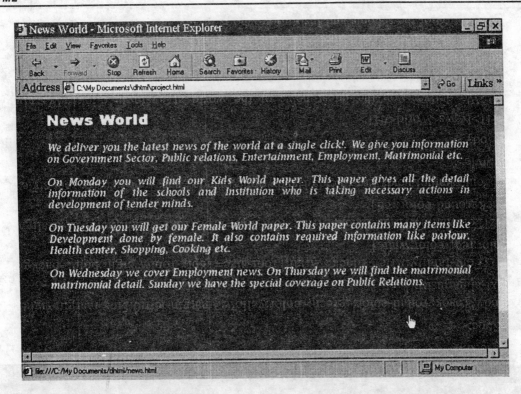

This page describes about different news topic. An image is linked with current.html page.

Code :

```
<Html>
<Head>
<Title>News World</Title>
</Head>
<Style>
Body{background-color:skyblue; color:red; margin-left:0.4in; margin-right:0.4in }
Table{font-size:18pt; align:justify}
Td.change{background-color:blue; color:white; text-align:justify}
</Style>
<Body>
<Table =0>
<Tr>
<Td bgcolor="yellow">Current Affairs</Td><Td bgcolor="blue">Kids World</Td>
<Td bgcolor="yellow">Entertainment</Td><Td bgcolor="blue">Employment</Td>
<Td bgcolor="yellow">Female World</Td>
</Tr>
```

```
</Table><Br><Br>
<Table>
<Tr>
<Td><img src="C:\My Documents\dhtml\new.bmp"></Td><Td class="change">If you
join us we will provide you various facilities. You will be getting current news on any
field. Any special auctions given by any company will be mailed to you. Your kids will
get a chance of joining at our games club. In summer and winter holidays you will get
fabulous discount from STOC - World Famous Travel & Tours company.<Br>
<Span Style="font-size:20; background-color:red">WE OFFER FREE MAIL
FACILITY.</Span>
</Td>
</Tr>
</Table><Br>
<A href="C:\my documents\dhtml\current.html"><img align="right" src="c:\my
documents\dhtml\click.bmp"></A>
</Body>
</Html>
```

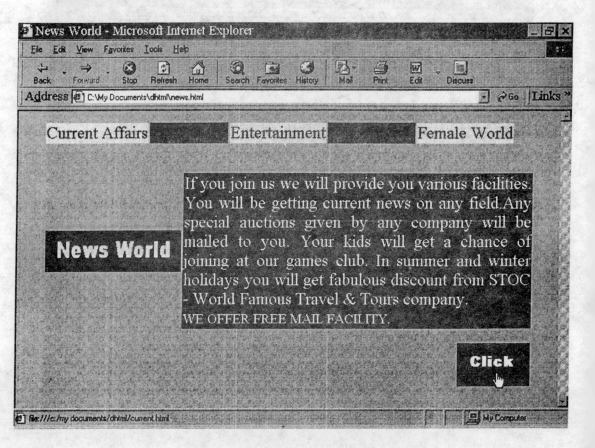

This page describes about different news on Current Affairs. An image is linked with kid.html page.

Code :

```
<HTML>
<Head>
<Title>Current Affairs</Title>
</Head>
<Style>
Body{background-color:purple; color:yellow; margin-left:0.5in; margin-right:0.5in}
H1{font-size:20; background-color:yellow; color:blue; text-align:center}
H2{font-size:18; color:white; text-align:right}
UL{font-size:14}
P{text-align:justify; border-style:double; border-color:white}
</Style>
<Body>
<H1>Current Affairs</H1>
<H2>Today's Headlines</H2>
<Ul>
<Li>Naga Talks in Osaka
<Li>Omar mystery deepens; search for Osama on
<Li>Made in India by China for Taliban
<Li>Tangled webs they weave
<Li>Kidnap accused shot
<Li>Angry investors take to the streets
</Ul>
<H2>Weather</H2>
<P>Mainly clear sky. Minimum temperature likely to be around 17<sup>0</sup>C.
Yesterday's Readings:-
Maximum temperature up to 6.30 p.m. was 29.8<sup>0</sup>C(+3)
Minimum temperature up to 8.30 a.m. was 15.5<sup>0</sup>C(+3)
Relative Humidity: Maximum 97% minimum 42%.
Relative humidity at 6.oo a.m. 91%(+15) and at 5.00 p.m. 65%(0)
Rainfall:nill. Sun sets today at 4.52 p.m. rises tomorrow at 6.00 a.m. Moon sets today
at 1.00 p.m., rises at 1.24 a.m. New moon on 15 December.
<A Href="c:\my documents\dhtml\kid.html"><Img align="right" src="C:\Program
Files\Microsoft Visual Studio\Common\Graphics\Icons\Misc\misc28.ico"></A>
</P>
</Body>
</Html>
```

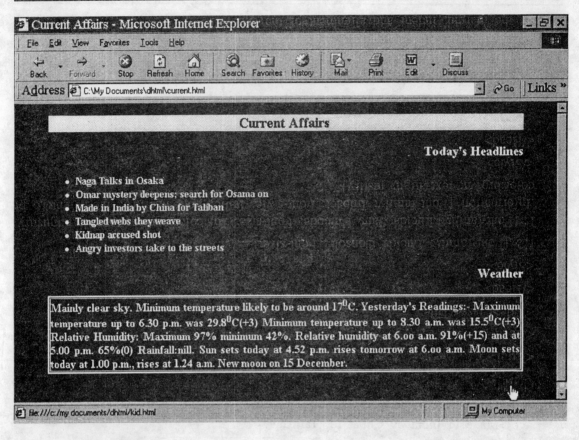

This page describes different information for kids. An image is linked with Entertainment.html page.

Code :

```
<Html>
<Head>
<Title>Kids</Title>
</Head>
<Style>
Body{background-color:gray; margin-left:0.5in; margin-right:0.5in}
P{border-style:groove; background-color:red; color:white; font-size:20}
</Style>
<Body>
<center><img src="C:\my documents\dhtml\new1.bmp"></center>
<H2>Kids enjoy your holidays with your favourite cartoons.</H2>
<P>Peanuts CD worth Rs.400/-.</P>
<P>Zorro CD worth Rs.500/-.</P>
<P>Archie CD worth Rs.450/-.</P>
<P>Dennis the Menace CD worth Rs.560/-.</P>
```

```
<A Href="C:\my documents\dhtml\entertainment.html"><Img align="right"
src="C:\Program Files\Microsoft Visual
Studio\Common\Graphics\Icons\misc\lighton.ico">
</A>
</Body>
</Html>
```

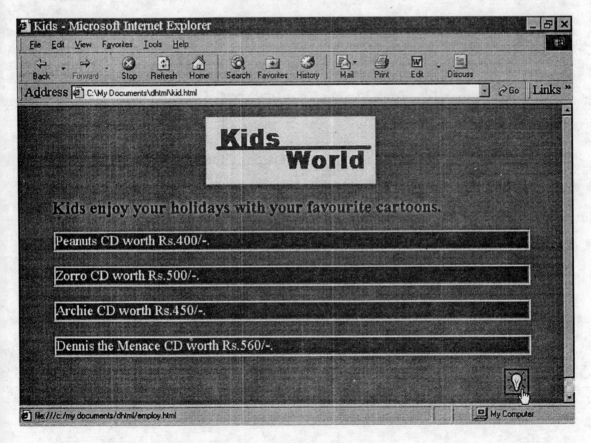

This entertainment page describes the program details. An image is linked with Employ.html page.

Code :

```
<Html>
<Head>
<Title>Entertainment</Title>
</Head>
<Style>
Body{background-color:pink; color:red}
H1{font-size:28; text-align:center}
```

```
P{font-size:25}
Table{font-size:20; background-color:lightyellow}
</Style>
<Body>
<H1>Entertainment</H1>
<P>
Enjoy with different programs this week. <Br><Br>
<Table>
<Tr>
<Td>Antakshari</Td><Td>5.30.p.m.</Td><Td>Special Guest Anupam Shukla</Td>
</Tr>
<Tr>
<Td>Movie</Td><Td>9.00.p.m.</Td><Td>Starring Monty & Reshma</Td>
</Tr>
<Tr>
<Td>Cartoon Show</Td><Td>10.a.m.</Td><Td>Story of Tintiny</Td>
</Tr>
<Tr>
<Td>News</Td><Td>12.noon.</Td><Td>All the latest news</Td>
</Tr>
<Tr>
<Td>Comedy Show</Td><Td>1.30 p.m.</Td><Td>Presented by Jony</Td>
</Tr>
<Tr>
<Td>Fitness</Td><Td>1.30 p.m.</Td><Td>Renuka Desai will show exercises.</Td>
</Tr>
</Table>
<Hr>
<A Href="C:\my documents\dhtml\employ.html"><Img align="right" src="C:\Program
Files\Microsoft Visual Studio\Common\Graphics\Icons\Writing\Book04.ico"></A>
</Body>
</Html>
```

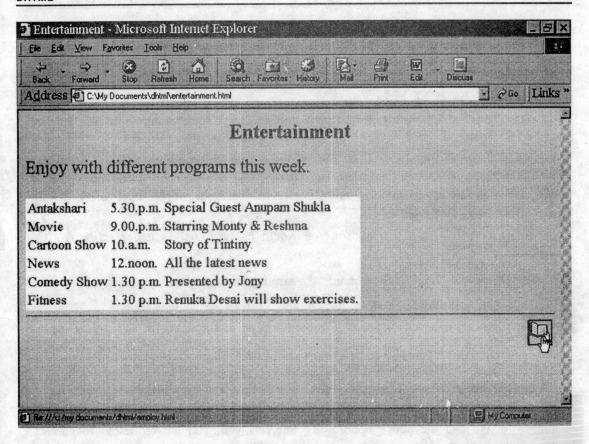

This page describes the employment details. An image is linked with Female.html page.

Code :

```
<Html>
<Head>
<Title>Employment</Title>
</Head>
<Style>
Body{margin-left:0.4in;  margin-right:0.4in}
P{font-size:22;  font-style:verdana, MS Sans Serif;  font-weight:bold;  background-color:black;  color:white;  text-align:center}
.job{font-size:17;  font-style:oblique;  font-weight:bold}
.intro{font-size:16;  font-style:Lucida Sans, Lucida Handwriting;  font-weight:bold;  background-color:lightyellow;  color:red;  text-align:justify}
.benefit{font-size:14;  font-style:Lucida Handwriting,Lucida Sans;  font-weight:bold;  background-color:lightgreen;  color:red;  text-align:justify}
```

```
Ul{font-size:12; font-weight:bold}
</Style>
<Body>
<P>Have A Job Yet Be Free</P>
```

<P class="intro">Jahindra Life Insurance Company Ltd., a joint venture between Jahindra and PIK Finance is looking for Life Advisors to market their product.

Jahindra is one of India's leading financial services groups, with asstes worth over Rs.2,000 crore. PIK is an international financial services group with 100 years of experience in life insurance and assets under management worth Rs.10 crore (as on 31st December 2001).</P>

<P class="benefit">As a life advisor you would be benefited as under :</P>
<Ul>
<Li>Flexibility of your working hours & earnings as per your requirement.

<Li>You can continue with your present job. May be as second source of earnings.

<Li>Entitlement to a percentage of the premium as commission till the policy are in force.

<Li>Always personal training.</Ul>
<P class="benefit">

If you are 10 + 2, or agent of other financial organisation or a retired individual or housewife, etc and the above opportunity interests you, you are requested to contact our office between 10a.m.to 5p.m.on 14th Jan.2001.

venue : 2nd floor, Block-C. Park St.Kolkata - 700 016.<P>

<P class="job">

Knowledge of Finance and ability to relate people will be a added advantage.</P>

<A Href="C:\my documents\dhtml\female.html"><Img align="right" src="C:\Program Files\Microsoft Visual Studio\Common\Graphics\Icons\Misc\Face05.ico"></A>

```
</Body>
</Html>
```

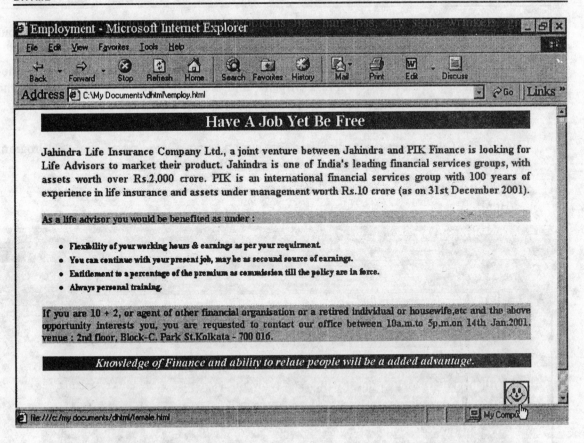

This page describes beauty tips for female. An image is linked with Project.html page i.e. Home page of our project.

Code :

```
<Html>
<Head>
<Title>Female</Title>
</Head>
<Style>
Body{background-color:yellow; margin-Left:0.7in; margin-Right:0.7in}
H1{Font-size:28; text-align:center; background-color:red; color:yellow}
P{Font-size:20; text-align:justify; background-color:brown; color:yellow}
</Style>
<Body>
<H1>Beauty Tips</H1>
<P>For three days our web site will give you information on differnt beauty tips. You
will also find solution on differnet problems like hair loss, dry skin, wrinkels, grey hair,
dandruff etc. </P>
```

<P>We will provide you a diet chart and the nutrition table which will control your diet. Balanced diet is very important to maintain the body. </P>

<P>You can mail us your problem at <Span style="text-decoration:underline; Color:blue">Femaleworld@vsnl.net</Span> and we will mail back to you with the solution of your problem.

</P>

<A Href="C:\my documents\dhtml\project.html"><Img align="right" src="C:\Program Files\Microsoft Visual Studio\Common\Graphics\Icons\Misc\House.ico"></A>

</Body>

</Html>

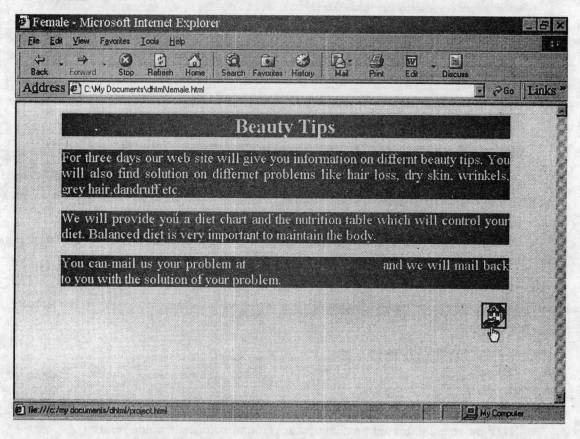

❋ ❋ ❋

JAVA SCRIPT

15

Java Script

Introduction

Now you are well conversant with HTML & DHTML, but you would have noticed that all the pages you have created is static. While browsing the net you have seen dynamic web pages, which interacts with the users. Now a day's users are not fascinated by simple scrolling text or by the background colors. They like to browse the sites, which interacts with the users input and they like to get the customized output in basis of their input. You might have seen while browsing the net once you click on submit button, (say you are filling a form) a page opens delivering you the proper message regarding the submission of data. More over in online transaction validation is a common feature.

Netscape Communication Corporation who also developed the Web Browser – Netscape Navigator, developed JavaScript.

⇨ Using Java Script you can add scrolling and changing messages in the status bar of the Browser.

⇨ You can set validation while working with form elements.

⇨ You can display messages using alert, confirm dialogs.

⇨ Animate images using different mouse events.

⇨ Detecting the Browser in use and display different contents for different browsers.

⇨ Working with plug-ins.

What is Validation?

Validation is necessary to check the valid user. Sometimes due to validation it shows error message when the user fills the form improperly (say for not filling a field or might be for filling a textual field with number). This protects the data. This kind of interaction is possible with a scripting language like Java Script.

How you can navigate?

So now we will step forward to create web pages, using Java Script. Using Java Scripts we can create interactive web pages which response on users interaction. We can include navigational features, which help the users to navigate between the numbers of pages. Sometimes you would have noticed that after selecting an option from the list or say after clicking on a button a new page opens.

How to display message?

You can display message using alert, confirm dialogs. Using prompt we can collect information from the users in Java Script.

Difference between Java Script and Java

Sun Microsystems had developed Java programming language, which is used to create applets and programs to execute in web browsers. After compilation the code is produced for virtual machines. Later the code gets interpreted in the web browser. For this reason on different platforms the output appears same. For ex. same output in PCs and in Macintoshes which is not possible in JavaScript.

There are some similarities between Java and Java Script but actually Java Script is used to add different functionality like user interaction, validation etc in the HTML file which helps the web authors to create web pages in less time and using less effort.

Java Scripts uses simple text while Java applets should be compiled into class files for using it in web page.

Java applets have its own shape i.e. rectangle while Java Script formats the web according to your choice.

Java applets can be used for creating complex programs but i.e. not possible in Java Script.

How to begin?

Java Script is very flexible because it can be embedded between the HTML tags in a HTML file. It has the same extension .htm or .html. Moreover the Java Script enabled browser interprets the language as it happens in a HTML file so further compilation is not required.

How to edit?

Editing Java Script is also very easy. Just open the editor, make the require changes and then save it. Once you upload the page in the Browser the changes effect in or press the Refresh button if the page is already uploaded.

How Java Script works

JavaScript mainly based on Object Oriented Programming and you can create event driven programming.

When the HTML page gets upload in the browser it recognize each objects of the HTML page, but later on after finishing the loading it cannot recognize each objects individually.

But to work with each object and to create functionality it is necessary for the Browser to recognize the objects. JavaScript enabled browser allows to recognize each object. With the help of JavaScript you can create interactive web pages using the object properties, methods and by creating functions. This is possible because the browser uses DOM.

A brief description on DOM (Document Object Model)

DOM works in descending hierarchy.

The first position of the DOM is the Navigator or you can say the Browser.

The Next position of the DOM is the Browser Window i.e. Internet Explorer, Netscape Navigator etc.

Then comes the position of document i.e. the HTML document that contains a Form.

And at the end is the Form where the elements are available like textbox, textarea, buttons etc.

So by maintaining the descending hierarchy of DOM the JavaScript enabled browser identifies the elements of the web page, because all are bound with DOM.

While adding JavaScript in the HTML document we have to state the script language as JavaScript. The scripting begins with the <Script> tag and ends with the </Script> tag.

<Script Language="JavaScript">

.....

......

</Script>

According to your requirement you can place the script in the <Header> in the <Body> or inside the <Html> tag of the Html document.

Embedding JavaScript in HTML

Follow the code, which shows embedding of JavaScript

Code :

```
<Html>
<Head>
<Title>Java Script</Title>
</Head>
<Body Bgcolor="Lightblue">
<Font size=5>
<Center><H1>Java Script</H1></Center><Br><Br>
<Script Language="JavaScript">
```

```
document.write("<B><I>Let's start with Java Script</B></I>")
</Script>
</Body>
</Html>
```

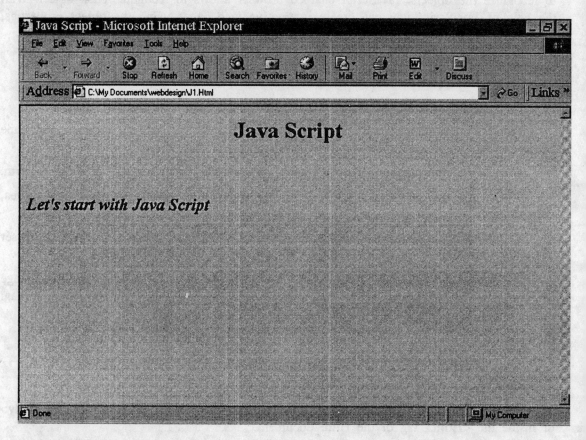

Here I have added a text using document.write("Let's start with Java Script").

Versions of Java Script

Java Script began in Netscape 2.0. The version details are as follows.

The original version 1.0 – Supported by Netscape 2.0 and in Internet Explorer 3.0

Version 1.1 is supported by Netscape 3.0 and in Internet Explorer 4.0.

Version 1.2 is supported by Netscape 4.0 and in Internet Explorer 4.0.

And version 1.3 is supported by Netscape 4.5.

✷ ✷ ✷

16

Describing the Operators

In JavaScript you can use various types of operators like

⇨ Arithmetic
⇨ Logical
⇨ Comparison
⇨ Conditional
⇨ String
⇨ Assignment
⇨ Bit Manipulation

Arithmetic operators are the simple operators used by us for mathematical calculations.

Operator	Description
+	Addition
-	Subtraction
*	Multiplication
/	Division
%	Modulus(Calculates the remainder of dividing two integers)
++	Increment and then return value (or return value and then increment)
--	Decrement and then return value (or return value and the decrement)

Logical Operators based on Boolean operands.

Operator	Description
&&	Logical and
||	Logical or
!	Logical not

Comparison Operators compare between the values like

Operator	Description
==	Equal
===	Strictly Equal
!=	Not equal
!==	Strictly not equal
<	Less than
<=	Less than or equal
>	Greater than
>=	Greater than or equal

Conditional Operators

The Conditional Operators are - ? :
It takes three operands condition ? value1 : value2
If the condition matches it shows value1 else it shows value2

String Operators

String Operators are used for concatenation between the strings. For ex. "Java" + "Script" joins two strings together and creates JavaScript. So + does the string concatenation.

Assignment Operators

Operator	Description
=	Sets the variable on the left of the = operator to the value of the expression on its right.
+=	Increments the variable on the left of the += operator by the value of the expression on its right. When used with strings, the value to the right of the += operator is appended to the value of the variable on the left of the += operator.
-=	Decrements the variable on the left of the -=operator by the value of the expression on its right.
*=	Multiplies the variables on the left of the *= operator by the value of the expression on its right.
/=	Divides the variables on the left of the /= operator by the value of the expression on its right.
%=	Takes the modulus of the variable on the left of the %= operator using the value of the expression on its right.
<<=	Left shifts the variable on the left of the <<= operator using the value of the expression on its right.

>>=	Takes the sign-propagating right shift of the variable on the left of the >>= operator using the value of the expression on its right.
>>>=	Takes the zero-filled right shift of the variable on the left of the >>>= operator using the value of the expression on its right.
&=	Takes the bitwise and of the variable on the left of the &= operator using the value of the expression on its right.
!=	Takes the bitwise or of the variables on the left of the != operator using the value of the expression on its right.
^=	Takes the bitwise exclusive or of the variable on the left of the ^= operator using the value of the expression on its right.

Creating Functions

Now we will learn how to add functions in the script. Function should be defined and it should be compact with an opening brace and with an end brace. The browser locates the function by its opening brace and the end brace. In the previous example you have seen that using document.write, a simple text has been added. Now you can add the same text by creating a function.

Example

```
Function Start()
{
    document.write("<B><I>Let's start with Java Script</B></I>");
}
```

So when you will call the function it will display the text.

Now follow the code where you will find two user defined functions one is goto() which opens a new site when the user clicks on the New Site button. The other one is changeColor() which changes the background color in the onload event.

Note. See the List of Event Handlers to get the information about onload event.

Code :

```
<Html>
<Head>
<Title>Onload</Title>
</Head>
<Script Language="JavaScript">
function goto()
{
    open("C:/My Documents/javascript/new.html","w1");
}
```

```
function changeColor()
{
    document.bgColor="lightgreen";
}
</Script>
<Body onLoad='changeColor()'>
<form name=f1
<H2>Creating User defined functions</H2>
<Hr color="red">
<P>Click on the button "New Site" to open a web page.</P>
<Hr color="blue">
<Input type="button" value="New Site" onClick='goto()'>
</Form>
</Body>
</Html>
```

Code of new.html

```
<Html>
<Head>
<Title>New page</Title>
</Head>
<Body background="C:\My Documents\fuji.jpg">
<H1>Welcome at our site</H1>
</Body>
</Html>
```

Hiding Scripts

Users having incompatible or old browser do not response the script. Sometime it displays the web in a text format without performing the work. So to avoid this problem enclose the script within the comment tags. It begins with < — and ends with — >.

Follow the code, which shows the use of comment tag

Code :

```
<Html>
<Head>
<Title>Onload</Title>
</Head>
<Script Language="JavaScript">
< —
function goto()
{
open("C:/My Documents/javascript/new.html","w1");
}
function changeColor()
{
document.bgColor="lightgreen";
}
// — >
</Script>
<Body onLoad='changeColor()'>
<form name=f1>
<H2>Creating User defined functions</H2>
<Hr color="red">
<P>Click on the button "New Site" to open a web page.</P>
<Hr color="blue">
<Input type="button" value="New Site" onClick='goto()'>
</Form>
</Body>
</Html>
```

Code of new.html

```
<Html>
<Head>
<Title>New page</Title>
</Head>
<Body background="C:\My Documents\fuji.jpg">
<H1>Welcome at our site</H1>
</Body>
</Html>
```

<NOSCRIPT> tag

Another solution is to use <NOSCRIPT> tag, which hides the script from older browser and does not display the script. The Java Script compatible browsers ignore the <NOSCRIPT> tag and perform the work correctly. One thing you must remember i.e. though Netscape 2.0 supports Java Script does not support the <NOSCRIPT> tag.

What are Objects?

What you see is an object and it is present in the computer world too. So, now lets work with objects. It contains two things methods and properties.

⇨ It is the collection of properties that contain the data

⇨ Methods to act on that data to perform the operations

In Java Script you will find various objects like document object and it has write() method, window object and it has alert(), confirm() etc. method.

Java Script supports three kinds of Objects:

Built-in objects . There are many built-in objects found in JavaScript like array, string, data, math etc.

Browser Objects. It represents various Browser objects and the HTML document like alert(), confirm(), prompt etc.

Custom Objects. It represents the object created by you.

Handling Events

Java Script handles events using the Event Handlers. When an event occurs the Event Handler says the Browser to perform the work. Say when the button will be clicked the alert message box appears. So the Event Handler says the Browser to show the message box.

First you have to define the object and then specify it in the Event Handler tag. Java Scripts defines event on different objects of the web, which includes windows, links, images, image maps, form elements etc.

Study the table, which displays the list of events defined by JavaScript that are common to Navigator and Internet Explorer.

HTML Element & Tags	Event	Description
all elements	mouseMove	When you move the mouse.
link (<A>....</A>)	click	When you click the mouse on a link.
	dbClick	When you double-click the mouse on a link.
	mouseDown	When you press the mouse.
	mouseUp	When you release the mouse.
	mouseOver	When you move the mouse over the link.
	mouseOut	When you move the mouse out of the link.
	keyDown	When you press a key.
	keyUp	When you release a key.
	keyPress	When you press and release a key.
image (<img>)	abort	This event aborts the image while loading.
	error	An error occurs while loading of an image.
	load	An image gets loaded and displayed.
	keyDown	When you press a key.
	keyUp	When you release a key.
	keyPress	When you press and release a key.
area (<Area>)	mouseOver	When you move the mouse over the client-side area of image map.
	mouseOut	When you move the mouse out of image map area
	dblClick	When you double-click on the image map area.
document body (<Body>....</Body>)	click	When you click the mouse on the body.
	dblClick	When you double-click the mouse on the body.
	keyDown	When you press a key.
	keyUp	When you release a key.
	keyPress	When you press and release a key.
	mouseDown	When you press the mouse.
	mouseUp	When you release the mouse.
window, frameset, frame (<Body>...</Body>) (<Frameset>...</Frameset>) (<Frame>...</Frame>)	blur	A window loses the current input focus.

HTML Element & Tags	Event	Description
	error	Error occurs while loading the window.
	focus	The window receives the current input focus.
	load	The loading of the window is completed.
	unload	When the user exits the window.
	move	When window is moved.
	resize	When the window is resized.
	dragdrop	When the user drops an object onto the window.
form (<Form>....</Form>)	submit	When the user submits the form.
	reset	When the user resets the form.
text field (<Input type= "text">	blur	When the text field loses its current input focus.
	focus	When the text field receives its current input focus.
	change	When the text field is modified and loses the current input focus.
	select	When the text is selected within the text field.
password field (<Input type= "password">)	blur	When the field loses its current input focus.
	focus	When the field receives its current input focus.
textarea (<Textarea>..</Textarea>)	blur	When the textarea loses the current input focus.
	change	When the text field is modified and loses the current input focus.
	select	When the text is selected within the text field.
	keyDown	When you press a key.
	keyUp	When you release a key.
	keyPress	When you press and release a key.
button (<Input type= "button">)	click	When button is clicked.
	blur	When the button loses the input focus.
	focus	When the button gains the input focus.
	mouseDown	When the user presses the left button of the mouse.
	mouseUp	When the user releases the left button of the the mouse.

HTML Element & Tags	Event	Description
submit (<Input type= "submit">)	click	When the submit button is clicked.
	blur	When the submit button loses the input focus.
	focus	When the submit button gains the input focus.
reset (<Input type= "reset">)	click	When the reset button is clicked.
	blur	When the reset button loses the input focus.
	focus	When the reset button gains the input focus.
radio button (<Input type= "radio">)	click	When the radio button is clicked.
	blur	When the radio button loses the input focus.
	focus	When the radio button gains the input focus.
checkbox (<Input type= "checkbox">)	click	When the checkbox button is clicked.
	blur	When the checkbox button loses the input focus.
	focus	When the checkbox button gains the input focus.
file upload (<Input type= "file">)	blur	When a file upload form element loses the input focus.
	change	When the user selects a file to be uploaded.
	focus	When a file upload form element gains the input focus.
selection (<select>...</select>)	blur	When the selection element loses the current input focus.
	change	When the selection element is modified and loses the current input focus.
	focus	When the element receives the current input focus.

Working with Events

Java Scripts executes the code in response of the particular event. Study the example, which shows the click event of the mouse.

Code :

```
<Html>
<Head>
<Title>Click Event </Title>
</Head>
<Body>
<Script Language="JavaScript">
function change()
{
    document.bgColor="yellow";
}
</Script>
<H1>Working with Events</H1>
<hr>
<Input type="button" value="Change" onClick='change()'>
</Body>
</Html>
```

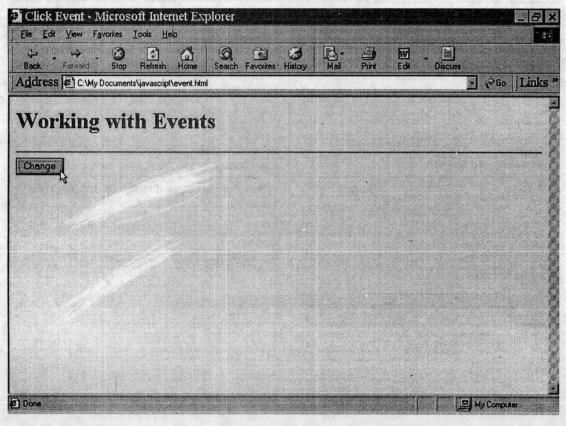

In this example you will find the background color changes from white to yellow when the user clicks the change button i.e. the click event.

List of Event Handlers

This table displays the list of event-handling attributes of the HTML elements. This table will guide you to work with the event handlers.

Event Handler	Occurs when:
onAbort	The loading of an image is aborted as a result of user action.
onBlur	A document, window, frame set, or form element loses current input focus.
onChange	A text field, text area, file-uploaded field or selection is modified and loses the current input focus.
onClick	A link, client-side image map area or document is clicked.
onDblClick	A link, client-side image map area or document is double clicked.
onDragDrop	A dragged object is dropped in a window or frame.
onError	An error occurs during loading of an image, window or frame.
onFocus	A document, window, frame set or form element receives the current input focus.
onKeyDown	The user presses a Key
onKeyPress	The user presses and releases a Key
onKeyUp	The user releases a Key
onLoad	An image document or frame set is loaded.
onMouseDown	The user presses a mouse button.
onMouseMove	The user moves the mouse.
onMouseOut	The mouse is moved out of a link or an area of a client side image map.
onMouseOver	The mouse is moved over a link or an area of a client side image map.
onMouseUp	The user releases a mouse button
onReset	The user resets a form by clicking on the form's reset button
onResize	The user resizes a window or frame
onSelect	Text is selected in a text field or a text area
onSubmit	The user presses a form's submit button
onUnload	The user exits a document or frame set.

<Input type=button value="Change" onClick='onAlert()'>

You have to incorporate the Event Handler as an attribute in the Html tag ie. onClick is an Event Handler. Then you have to write the JavaScript statement inside the quotes i.e. 'onAlert()'. Generally it contains the function name, which is created separately.

For Example

```
Function onAlert()
{
    alert('Are You Sure');
}
```

You can identify Java Script event handlers easily because it has a prefix "on" added. Another thing you have to remember i.e. for creating an event handler you don't require a <script> tag. Lets call the onMouseOver event handler in a link, which will display an alert message.

Follow the code, which shows onMouseOver event

Code :

```
<Html>
<Head>
<Title>Event Handlers</Title>
</Head>
<Body>
<H1>Working with Event Handlers</H1>
<Hr color="red">
<Font size="4">
<P>Hold the mouse over the link and see what happens.</P>
<P><A Href="C:\my documents\javascript\eventlist.html"
onMouseOver="alert('An example to show you onMouseOver Event
Handler')">Working with onMouseOver event handler - hold the mouse here.</A>
</P>
</Body>
</Html>
```

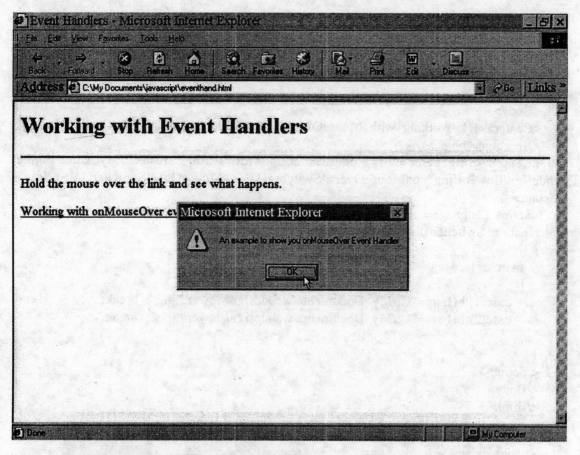

Working with various Java Script events

Now you have an idea about events and the event handlers. So lets work with various events of Java Script.

Mouse Events

There are various mouse events. There are many event handlers, which detect the mouse actions like onMouseOver, onMouseOut, onMouseUp, onMouseDown.

Working with Over and Out event

onMouseOver. Works when the mouse pointer is over an object, link, image etc.

onMouseOut. Works when the mouse pointer is out of the object's border i.e. away from the object. It is generally called when onMouseOver handler is used.

Follow the code, which shows the MouseOver and MouseOut events.

Code :

```html
<Html>
<Head>
<Title>Switcher</Title>
</Head>
<Body>
<Center><H1>Working with MouseOver & MouseOut events</H1></Center>
<Hr color="blue">
<Center><Img name="bt1" height="200" width="200" src="C:/My Documents/
webdesign/flower4.jpg" onMouseOver='Switcher(1)' onMouseOut='Switcher(2)'></Img>
</Center>
<Script Language="JavaScript">
function Switcher(place)
{
  switch(place)
  {
     case(1):bt1.src="C:/My Documents/webdesign/flower3.jpg"; break;
     case(2):bt1.src="C:/My Documents/webdesign/flower4.jpg"; break;
  }
}
</Script>
</Body>
</Html>
```

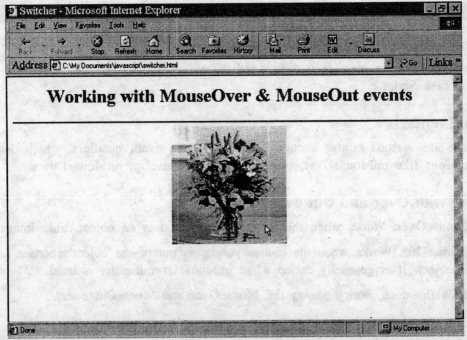

MouseOver –When the mouse pointer is over the image

MouseOut – When the mouse pointer is out of the image

Working with Up and Down event

onMouseDown. Works when the mouse button is pressed.

onMouseUp. Works when the mouse button is released. Actually Up and down events works simultaneously.

Follow the code, which shows the MouseUp and MouseDown events.

Code :

```
<Html>
<Head>
<Title>Switcher</Title>
</Head>
<Body>
<Center><H1>Working with MouseUp & MouseDown events</H1></Center>
<Hr color="blue">
<Center><Img name="bt1" height="200" width="200" src="C:/My Documents/
webdesign/flower2.jpg" onMouseDown='Switcher(1)' onMouseUp='Switcher(2)'>
</Img></Center>
```

```
<Script Language="JavaScript">
function Switcher(place)
{
  switch(place)
  {
    case(1):bt1.src="C:/My Documents/webdesign/flower1.jpg";
    document.bgColor="orange";
    break;
    case(2):bt1.src="C:/My Documents/webdesign/flower2.jpg";
    document.bgColor="white";
    break;
  }
}
</Script>
</Body>
</Html>
```

MouseDown – When the mouse button is pressed

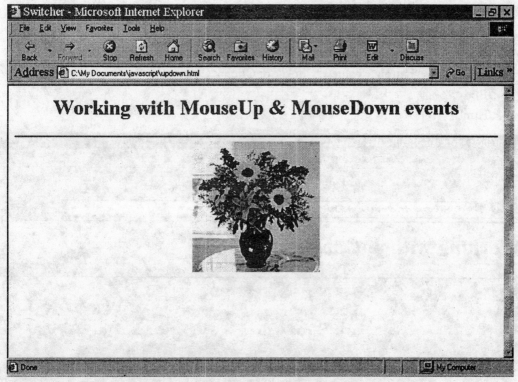

MouseUp – When the mouse button is released

Working with Click Events

Actually MouseDown and MouseUp is the two parts of click event. It is a very common event. Follow the example, which changes the background color after showing a confirmation message by calling the function in the onClick event of the mouse.

Code :

```
<Html>
<Head>
<Title>OnClick</Title>
</Head>
<Body>
<Script Language="JavaScript">
function Change()
{
    confirm("Are you sure! This will change your backround color");
    document.bgColor="pink";
}
```

```
</Script>
<H1>Working with onClick event</H1>
<Hr color=red>
<Input type="button" value="Click" onClick='Change()'>
</Body>
</Html>
```

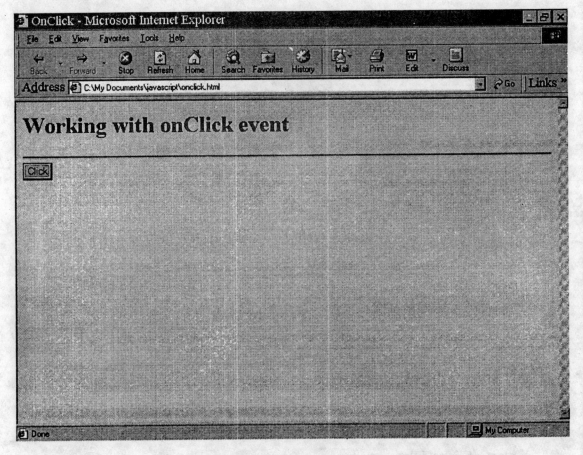

When the user clicks the button the onClick event calls the function and the confirm message appears.

When the user clicks the OK button of the confirm message the background color changes.

Working with Keyboard Events

In the previous versions JavaScript was not supporting the keyboard events but later JavaScript 1.2 and 1.3 can detect the keyboard actions. The main event handler is the keyPress, which occurs when a key is pressed and released simultaneously. As you have seen the events of MouseUp and MouseDown, same way we can detect KeyUp and KeyDown events. Using key events you can track which key the user had pressed. The event.which property stores the ASCII character code, which had been pressed.

Working with onLoad Events

This is a common event occurs when the loading of the page finishes from the server. It is related with the document object and to define it you require an event handler in the <Body> tag.

Follow the code, which shows the alert message after the completion of loading.

Code :

```
<Html>
<Head>
<Title>Onload</Title>
</Head>
<Body onLoad="alert('Loading is complete');">
<H1>Working with onLoad event</H1>
<Hr color="red">
</Body>
</Html>
```

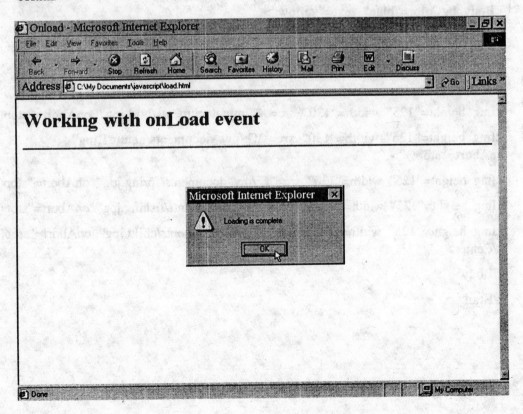

Working with onAbort event

This event mainly occurs when the loading of image is aborted i.e. while loading if the user clicks the stop button or changing the document. Follow the code which shows the alert message if the loading of image gets aborted.

Code :

```
<Html>
<Head>
<Title>onAbort</Title>
<Script Language="JavaScript">
function stop()
{
    alert("You have aborted the loading of image");
}
</Script>
</Head>
<Body bgColor="blue" text="yellow">
<Center>
<H1>Working with onAbort event</H1>
<Hr>
<Img height="125" width="130" src="C:/my documents/bird.jpg" onAbort="stop()">
<Img height="125" width="130" src="\C:/my documents/nature1.jpg"
onAbort="stop()">
<Img height="125" width="130" src="C:/my documents/spring.jpg" onAbort="stop()">
<Img height="125" width="130" src="C:/my documents/fishing.jpg" onAbort="stop()">
<Img height="125" width="130" src="C:/my documents/child.jpg" onAbort="stop()">
</Center>
</Body>
</Html>
```

The browser view shows all the images loaded but if the user aborts the loading by pressing the stop button or by calling a new document it will display this alert message.

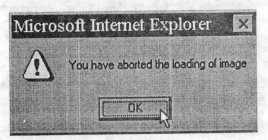

Working with onError event

While working with image you can display an error message if any error occurs while loading an image by using the onError event. Occasionally we have seen that error occurs if the browser cannot locate the image and you should inform the user by displaying proper message. Follow the code, which displays error message if error occurs while loading the image.

Code :

```
<Html>
<Head>
<Title>onAbort</Title>
<Script Language="JavaScript">
function stop()
{
   alert("An error occured while loading the image");
}
</Script>
</Head>
<Body bgColor="blue" text="yellow">
<Center>
<H1>Working with onError event</H1>
<Hr>
<Img height="125" width="130" src="C:/my documents/bird.jpg" onError="stop()">
<Img height="125" width="130" src="C:/my documents/nature1.jpg" onError="stop()">
<Img height="125" width="130" src="C:/my documents/spring.jpg" onError="stop()">
<Img height="125" width="130" src="C:/my documents/fishing.jpg" onError="stop()">
<Img height="125" width="130" src="C:/child.jpg" onError="stop()"></Center>
</Body>
</Html>
```

In this example the src property of one image is mentioned wrong for which onError event occurs and the error message gets displayed.

Note. The src property is changed just to give you a clear idea regarding onError event.

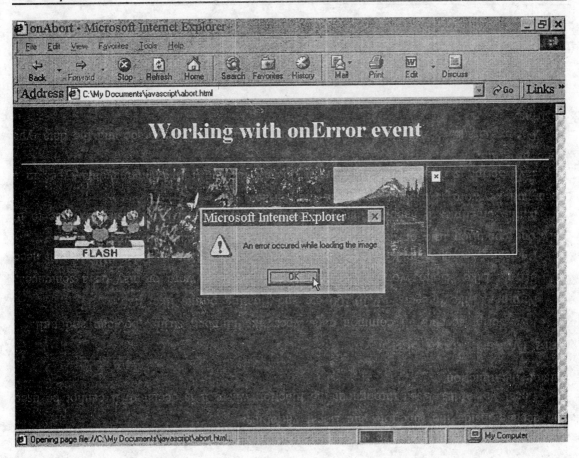

Working with onFocus & onBlur event

onFocus means when the element is getting the focus and onBlur means when the focus is removed. The example given shows the focus and blur event of two pages dropped in a frame. The color changes simultaneously onFocus and onBlur event.

Code for fram1.html :

```
<Html>
<Head>
<Title>Focus</Title>
<Script Language="JavaScript">
function yellow()
{
    document.bgColor="yellow";
}
function lightgreen()
```

```
{
    document.bgColor="lightgreen";
}
</Script>
</Head>
<Body onFocus="yellow()" onBlur="lightgreen()">
<H1>Working with onFocus and onBlur event</H1>
<P>When the page gets the focus the body color changes to yellow and when the
focus is removed i.e. onBlur event the color changes to light green.
</P>
</Body>
</Html>
```

Code for fram2.html:

```
<Html>
<Head>
<Title>Focus</Title>
<Script Language="JavaScript">
function lightyellow()
{
    document.bgColor="lightyellow";
}
    function lightblue()
{
    document.bgColor="lightblue";
}
</Script>
</Head>
<Body onFocus="lightyellow()" onBlur="lightblue()">
<H1>Working with onFocus and onBlur event</H1>
<Font size=4>
<P>When the page gets the focus the body color changes to lightyellow and when the
focus is removed i.e. onBlur event the color changes to light blue.
</P>
</Body>
</Html>
```

Now these two HTML document is displayed in a frameset.

Code :

```
<Html>
<Head>
<Title>Working with event</Title>
</Head>
<Frameset cols="50,50">
<Frame src="C:/my documents/javascript/fram1.html">
<Frame src="C:/my documents/javascript/fram2.html">
</Frameset>
</Html>
```

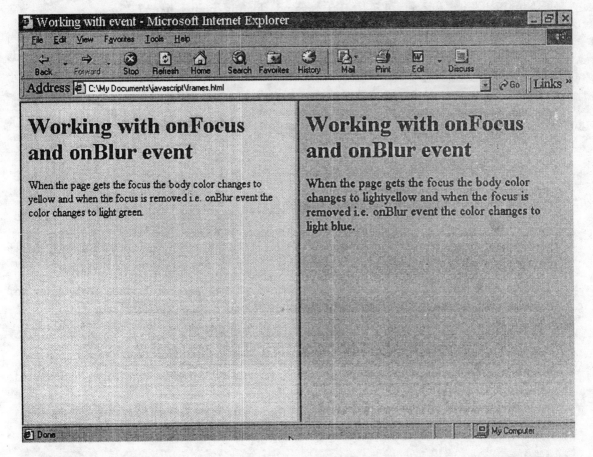

Variables

You require variables to assign values might be a text, number or an object. The variable you define should not contain any space and punctuation characters. You can only use letter and underscore. Try to give the variable name short because larger names might create confusion, as they are case sensitive. For ex. Total_sum is different from Total_Sum. In Java Script var keyword is used to declare a variable (i.e.var a) but when you assign value in a variable var keyword is not required (i.e. a = 30).

In Java Script you will find two types of variables.

Global Variables. Used throughout the script. It is declared inside the script tag. These variables can be used inside the script and inside the functions too. Generally the variables you declare inside the functions are Local variables.

Local Variables. Used throughout the function where it is declared. It cannot be used outside the function.

Data Types in Java Script

Java Script accepts all common data types like number, string, boolean and null.

Number. Like integers 1,7,10,100 etc and floating points like 7.25.

String. Like "Hello World". Consists text, might be a word or may be a sentence.

Boolean. As you may Know Boolean have two values True or False. Where you need only one condition true or false, there you should use Boolean data type.

Null. Sometimes it happens that you require a variable but can't assign a value to it. Then null keyword is used to represent the variable.

Java Script is friendly for all users it doesn't restrict from changing data types in a same program.

For ex. Grade = "A"; Here you are assigning A in a variable Grade and the data type is string.

Now For ex. Grade = 70.67; Here the data type of the same variable changed to number. This feature is valid in Java Script.

Conversion of Data Types

Some time you need to convert data from one type to another. For ex. from string to numeric format. Java Script offers two functions to solve this problem.

ParseInt(). This function converts a string to numeric type.

ParseFloat(). This function converts a string to floating-point number.

Both the functions will convert the string to numeric version. One thing you should remember that while converting it will consider only the numeric portions. For ex. if a variable contains a data 30 eggs, while converting it will store it will take only 30 and eggs will be omitted.

Calculating the String's Length

To find the total length of the variable you can use the length property. To find the length you need to write the variable name followed by .length. For ex. a= "Hello World"; and if you calculate the length it will display 11.

Follow the code, which calculates the length and displays after taking the input from the user.

Code :

```
<Html>
<Head>
<Script Language="JavaScript">
var name=prompt("Enter your name", "name");
</Script>
</Head>
<Body>
<H1>Working with Strings</H1>
<Hr color="red">
<Script Language="JavaScript">
document.write("<H2>Your name is "+name+"</H2>");
document.write("<H3>Total number of characters are   "+name.length+"</H3>");
</Script>
</Body>
</Html>
```

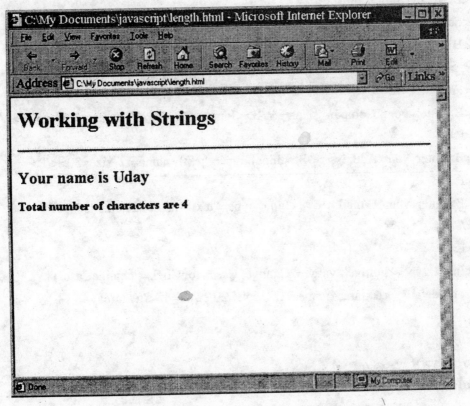

Converting the String's Case

Using the methods toUpperCase() and toLowerCase() converts the character to Uppercase or to Lowercase.

Follow the code where the string is converted to uppercase by the use of toUpperCase() in the click event of the button.

```html
<Html>
<Head>
<Title>Uppercase</Title>
<Script Language="JavaScript">
function changeCase()
{
   var upper=f1.t1.value+f1.t2.value+f1.t3.value;
   f1.ta.value=upper.toUpperCase();
}
</Script>
</Head>
<Body bgColor="pink">
<Form name=f1>
<H1>Changing the text to Uppercase</H1>
<P>
<Font size=4>
<B>Enter your Company Name:</B><Input type="text" name=t1 size=20></P>
<P>
<B>Enter your Address :</B><Input type="text" name=t2 size=30></P>
<P>
<B>Enter your E-mail:</B> <Input type="text" name=t3 size=30></P>
</P>
<P>
<Input type="button" value="Change Case" onClick="changeCase()">
Your details :<textarea name="ta" cols=20 rows=4></textarea>
</P>
</Form>
</Body>
</Html>
```

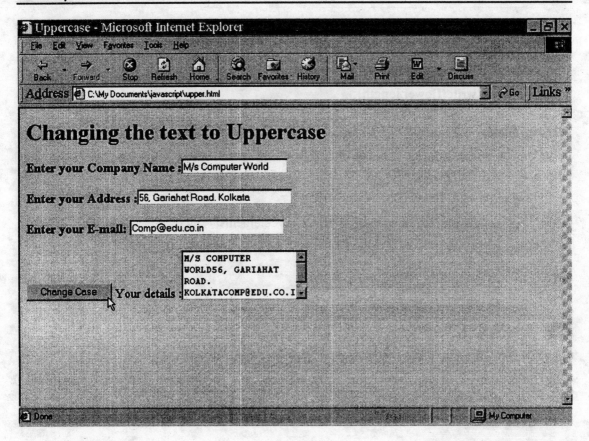

Creating Array

An array is an object, which stores sequence of values. The values are stored in the indexed location within the array. Array can contain strings, numbers, objects, or other types of data.

Numeric Array

For creating an array first you must declare the array. Follow the example – where you can store price of five flowers

flowers = new Array(5);

To assign values use brackets and an Index. Index starts from 0. So in this ex. you will find elements numbered from 0 to 4.

flower[0] = 5;
flower[1] = 6;
flower[2] = 8;
flower[3] = 10;
flower[4] = 15;

Like strings arrays have a length property. So to find the length you have to use flower.length, flower the array name followed by length. In this ex. the length is 5.

To print the length of the array code is

document.write(flower.length);

String Array

Unlike numeric array you can create a string array too. Follow the example, which stores names of five flowers

flowers = new Array(5);

Then assign the string values in the array elements

flowers[0] = "Lili";
flowers[1] = "Lotus";
flowers[2] = "Sunflower";
flowers[3] = "China Rose";
flowers[4] = "Rose";

So like this the array elements help you to work with strings.

Study the ex. which prints the array element in two different formats. Using join () joins each element of the array.

Code :

```
<Html>
<Head>
<Title>array</Title>
</Head>
<Body>
<Script language="JavaScript">
flowers=new Array(5);
flowers[0] = "Lili";
flowers[1] = "Lotus";
flowers[2] = "Sunflower";
flowers[3] = "China Rose";
flowers[4] = "Rose";
document.write(flowers[0]+"<Br>");
document.write(flowers[1]+"<Br>");
document.write(flowers[2]+"<Br>");
document.write(flowers[3]+"<Br>");
```

```
document.write(flowers[4]+"<Br>");
join_flower=flowers.join();
document.write("<H3>"+join_flower+"</H3>");
</Script>
</Body>
</Html>
```

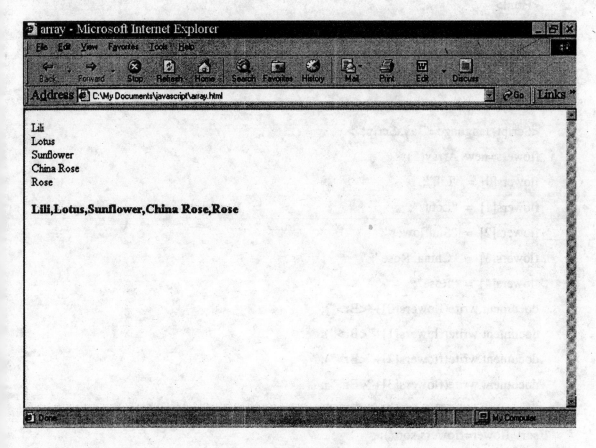

In this example you have seen the join() method in the same way you can split any string.

For example

Name= "M.Kar";

Parts=Name.split(" "); So the Parts array stores the string elements after splitting it.

Parts[0]= "M";

Parts[1]= "Kar";

Sorting an Array

As you have seen in the previous example joining and splitting of the string, same way you can sort it alphabetically or numerically.

Follow the example - which sorts the flowers name alphabetically.

Code :

```
<Html>
<Head>
<Title>sorting an array</Title>
</Head>
<Body>
<Script language="JavaScript">
flowers=new Array(5);
flowers[0] = "Lili";
flowers[1] = "Lotus";
flowers[2] = "Sunflower";
flowers[3] = "China Rose";
flowers[4] = "Rose";
document.write(flowers[0]+"<Br>");
document.write(flowers[1]+"<Br>");
document.write(flowers[2]+"<Br>");
document.write(flowers[3]+"<Br>");
document.write(flowers[4]+"<Br>");
sort_flower=flowers.sort();
document.write("<H3>"+sort_flower+"</H3>");
</Script>
</Body>
</Html>
```

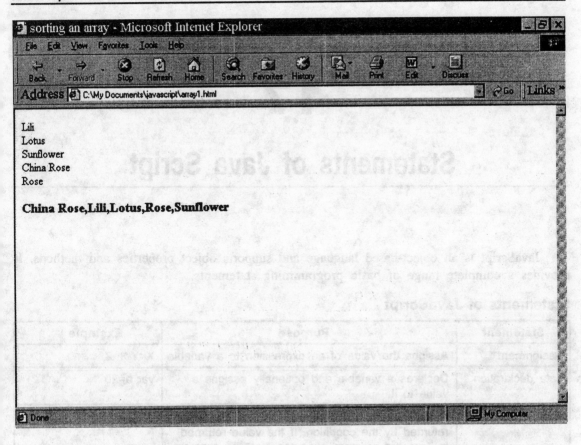

Note the array elements displayed in an alphabetical manner after sorting.

✳ ✳ ✳

17

Statements of Java Script

JavaScript is an object-based language and supports object properties and methods. It provides a complete range of basic programming statements.

Statements of JavaScript

Statement	Purpose	Example
Assignment	Assigns the value of an expression to a variable	X=Y + Z
data declaration	Declares a variable and optionally assigns a value to it.	var a=20

If	Program execution depends upon the value of returned by the condition. If the value returned is True the program executes else the program does not execute.	If (x>y)
		{
		  z=x
		}

Switch	Selects from a number of alternatives	switch (val)
		{
		  Case 1:
		  //first alternative break;
		  Case 2:
		  //second alternative break;
		  default
		  //default action
		}

While	Repeatedly executes a set of statements until a condition becomes false	while (x !=7)
		{
		  x%=n
		  -n
		}

For	Repeatedly executes a set of statements until a condition becomes false	for (I=0;I<7;++I)
		{
		  document.write(x[i])
		}

Statement	Purpose	Example

do while	Repeatedly executes a set of statements while a condition is true	do
		{
		// Statements
		}
		while (i>0)

label	Associates a label with a statement	LabelName: Statement
break	Immediately terminates a do while or for loop statement	if (x>y) break
continue	Immediately terminates the current iteration of a do, while or for statement	if (x>y) continue
function call	Invokes a function	x=abs(y)
return	Returns a value from a function call	return x*y

with	Identifies the default object	with (Math)
		{
		  d=PI * 2*r ;
		}

delete	Deletes an object property or an array element	delete a[3]
Method invocation	Invokes a method of an object	document.write ("Hello")

You have read the statements of Java Script. Now follow the program done by using the conditional statement. If-else is a conditional statement where the program performs a work if the condition satisfies else perform the other work if the condition dissatisfies.

Working with if-else statement

```
<Html>
<Head>
<Script language="JavaScript">
var Age=prompt("Enter your Age","Age");
</Script>
</head>
<Body>
<Script language="JavaScript">
if(Age>20)
{
  document.write("Adult")
}
```

```
else
{
  document.write("Young")
}
</Script>
</Body>
</Html>
```

So in this program a prompt appears first and takes the users input. Then it checks the condition whether the value is greater than 20 or not. If it is greater than 20 it displays Adult else it shows Young when the condition fails.

Working with Switch statement

When you need more than one condition then switch statement will solve the problem.

It starts with Switch statement and includes the value inside the brackets. For ex. Switch (Color)

The opening brace {and the closing brace} encloses the switch statement.

Conditions are written using the case statements, which compare with other case statements. In each case statement break is used to truncate the program so that after the condition of a case satisfies program should stop immediately.

Code :

```
<Html>
<Head>
<Title>Switch</Title>
<Script language="JavaScript">
var Color=prompt("Enter the Background Color","Color");
</Script>
</head>
<Body>
<H1>Changing Background Colors using switch</H1>
<Script language="JavaScript">
switch(Color)
{
    case "red":
    document.bgColor="red";
    break;
    case "green":
    document.bgColor="green";
```

```
        break;
        case "yellow":
        document.bgColor="yellow";
        break;
        default :
        window.alert("This "+Color+" is not available");
        }
    </Script>
    </Body>
    </Html>
```

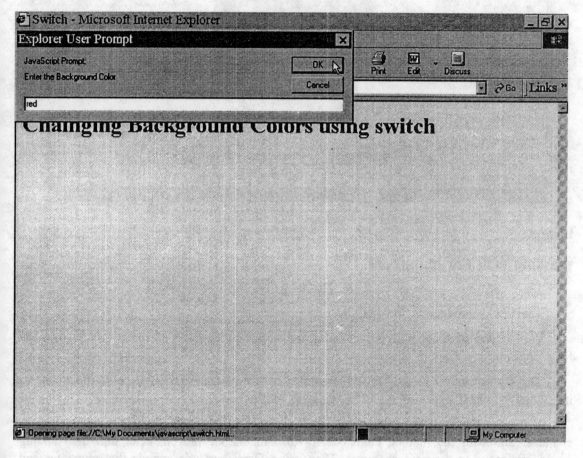

In this program the prompt asks for a color and checks with the condition and according to that it change the body background color. If the user request for a color, which is not mentioned in the case, then it shows the alert message mentioned in the default case.

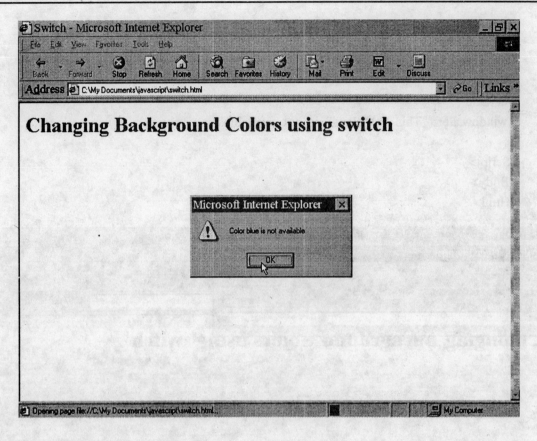

Loops

Working with For statement

There are three parameters in the For loop. For ex. for(i=0;i<l;i++)

The first parameter is the initialization part i.e i=0.

The second parameter i.e i<l contains the condition. So till the condition is true the loop continues.

The last parameter i.e i++ is the increment or decrement expression or you can say re-initialization which executes on each iteration of the loop.

Using the For loop in this program you can reach at the end of the string picking each character and with the method charCodeAt you can encode the character and then adding 1 you can move to the next character. Then using fromCharCode encode that character and then place it in the textbox. Creating a user defined function onChange() and using the click event of the button you can create this example.

Code :

```
<Html>
<Head>
<Title>Change</Title>
</Head>
<Body>
<Form name=f1 id=f1>
<Input type=text name=t1 id=t1>
<Input type=text name=t2 id=t2>
<input type=button value="Change" onclick='onChange()'>
<Script Language="JavaScript">
function onChange()
{
   s1=" ";
   l=0;
   b=0;
   s=f1.t1.value;
   l=s.length;
   for(i=0;i<l;i++)
   {
     a=s.charCodeAt(i);
     b=a+1;
     s1=s1+String.fromCharCode(b);
   }
   f1.t2.value=s1;
}
</Script>
</Body>
</Form>
</Html>
```

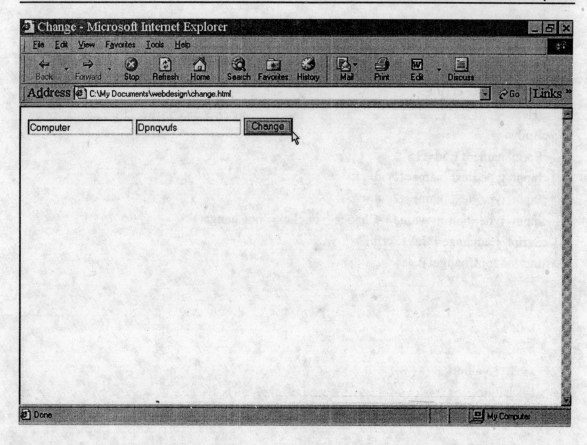

Working with While Statement

While statement performs the work till the condition is true. Here while statement checks whether the value given by the user is greater than 100 or not. When the condition satisfies, i.e. when the value is less than 100 it shows the square value of that number.

Code :

```
<Html>
<Head>
<Script language="JavaScript">
var N=0;
var Num=prompt("Enter a number within 100 to find the square","Num");
</Script>
</Head>
<Body>
<Font size=18>
<Script language="JavaScript">
while(Num<100)
```

```
{
    N=Num*Num;
    document.write("The Square value is "+N);
    break;
}
</Script>
</Body>
</Html>
```

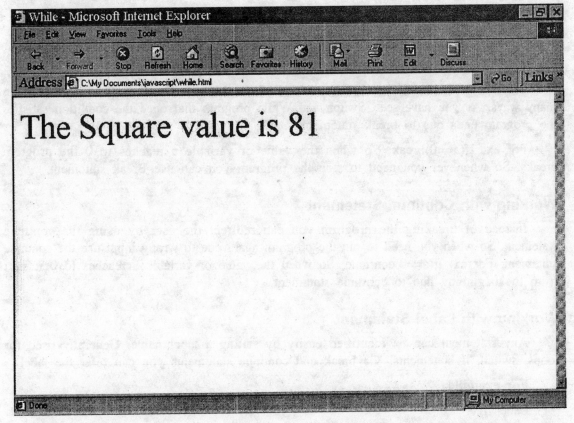

Like For loops you can use counter also in the while loops also, where the value increments or decrements till the while condition satisfies.

Say for ex.

```
While(a<10)
{
    a++;
    document.write(a);
}
```

So according to your choice and requirement you have to use the loop.

Working with Do while Statement

Do while loop executes at least once even if the condition fails. This is the difference between the while loop and do while loop.

Say for ex.
```
do
{
   a++;
   document.write(a);
}
While(a<10);
```

Working with Break Statement

Previously you have find break in the Switch program. Break helps the program in many ways. As you have seen Switch and While program that once the condition satisfies the program ends due to break statement.

For ex. If(a==0)break; So when the value of variable a reaches to 0 the program breaks. So whenever you need to stop the program you can use Break statement.

Working with Continue Statement

Instead of breaking the program you can redirect the user by using the continue statement. So when you need to run the program again due to wrong input use the continue statement. For ex. If(a==0)continue; So when the value of variable a reaches to 0 it start from the beginning due to continue statement.

Working with Label Statement

Any statement can be identified easily by setting a label name. Generally used for loops, switch, if statements. Via break and continue statements you can refer the label.

For example

Label 1:

A=B+C

18

Working with Browser Objects

Java Script performs a great work by manipulating the web browser. The script can manipulate web pages, windows and documents. It helps to load a page, open a page, create a window, open a window etc. The script helps to work with each part of web page. To work with the browser it uses the browser objects and as usual the browser objects have properties, which describes the web page and it maintains a method, which allow working with the part of a web page for ex. working with image, window etc. The browser objects maintain a hierarchy of parent and child objects. So while referring an object you need to write the parent object first followed by the child object and they are separated by dots. For ex. You want to change the background color so you will write document.bgColor= "red". No need of writing window.document.bgColor= "red"; because it existence is assumed so window prefix is not required when referring to its properties. When a web page gets loaded in the browser it automatically creates a number, which maps with DOM, which provides an access to the HTML objects.

List of Java Script objects created by Netscape Communicator.

Object Name	Use
Navigator	To access information about the browser that is executing the script.
Window	To access the browser window which includes the window or the frame.
Document	The document object accesses the document currently loaded. It refers to the content like Body, heading, and image of the HTML document.
Location	Location object represents an URL. You can create, access and modify an URL.
History	History object maintains a history of the URL's accessed within a window.
event	This object access the information about the occurrence of an event
Event	This object capitalized (Event) provides constants which helps to identify events.
Screen	This object access the information about the computer's screen like size, color depth in which the browser is running.

Working with Window Objects

While working with Window object you will find three types of methods for displaying messages and interacting with user. They are Confirm, Alert and Prompt dialogs. Confirm and alert dialogs are mainly used to display message whereas prompt dialogs helps to interact with the user.

Working with Confirm Dialog box

This display a dialog box, where you can set your confirm messages. The syntax is Confirm("Message"); It contains two buttons OK and Cancel.

Here the program shows the confirm dialog when the user clicks on the submit button.

Code :

```
<Html>
<Head>
<Title>Dialog</Title>
</Head>
<Form>
<Body Bgcolor="Lightpink" Text="Blue">
<center><H1>Application Form</H1></center>
<Br><Br>
<Font style="Arial" size=4>
Enter your Name :<Input type=text id=t1 size=20><Br><Br>
Enter your E-mail:<Input type=text id=t2 size=20><Br><Br>
Select your age:
<Select>
<Option>Above 18
<Option>20-30
<Option>30-40
<Option>Above 40
</Select><Br><Br>
<Input type=button name=b1 value="Submit" onClick='showcon()'>
<Script Language="JavaScript">
function showcon()
{
   confirm('Are you sure!');
}
</script>
</Form>
</Body>
</Html>
```

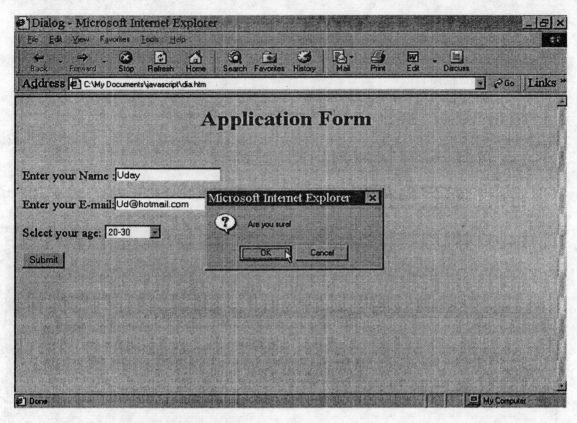

Working with Alert Dialog box

Though you have used Alert dialogs in the previous programs, follow this program where alert is used to display a message "Are you sure".

```
<Html>
<Head>
<Title>Quiz</Title>
</Head>
<Body  Bgcolor="Lightyellow">
<H1><center>Quiz  Contest</center></H1><Br><Br>
<Font  size=4>
<P>Select the right answer to you will be able to join with us at our show Quiz
Contest.</P>
<P>
<I>Monitor is a <Br>
<Input type="radio"  id=r1  name=r1="on">Visual  Display  Unit
<Input type="radio"  id=r2  name=r1="on">Central  Processing  Unit
</P>
```

```
<P>
<Input type="button" id=b1 value="Submit" onClick='onalert()'>
<Script Language="JavaScript">
function onalert()
{
    alert('Are You Sure');
}
</Script>
</Body>
</Html>
```

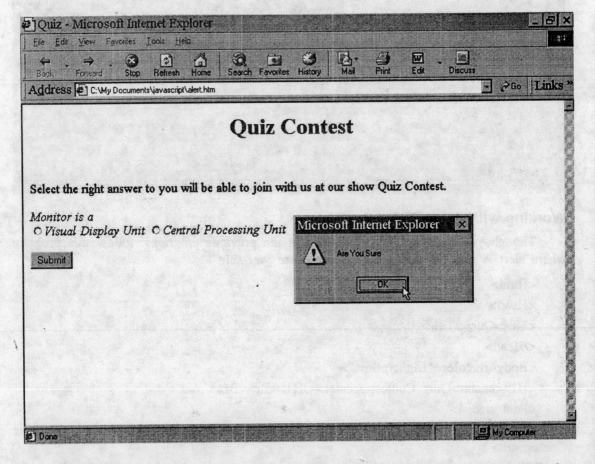

In this web page when the user clicks on the submit button the alert dialog displays asking the user " Are you sure!".

So now the use of Confirm dialog and Alert dialog is clear to you.

Working with Prompt dialog

Prompt dialog collects the input from the user and accordingly you can set the output. Though you have used prompt dialog before lets create a program, which verifies the valid user.

Code :

```
<Html>
<Head>
<Title>Prompt</Title>
<Script Language="JavaScript">
var pass =prompt("Enter the password","pass");
</Script>
</Head>
<Body>
<Script Language="JavaScript">
switch(pass)
{
  case "user":
  window.navigate("C:/My Documents/javascript/user.html","w1");
  break;
  default:
  document.write("<H2>Sorry! You are not a valid user - "+pass+"</H2>" );
}
</Script>
</Body>
</Html>
```

Code for user.Html:

```
<Html>
<Head>
<Title>User</Title>
</Head>
<Body bgcolor="pink">
<H1>Yes! you are a valid user</H1>
<Hr>
<Input type="button" value="Close" onClick="window.close();">
```

Now when the page gets uploaded in the browser the prompt appears.

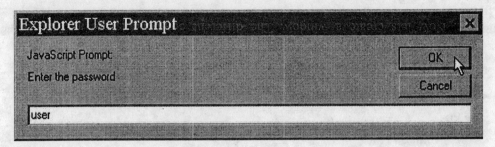

There are two cases one is when the user types user it opens the user.html page. The close button closes the window after displaying a confirm message.

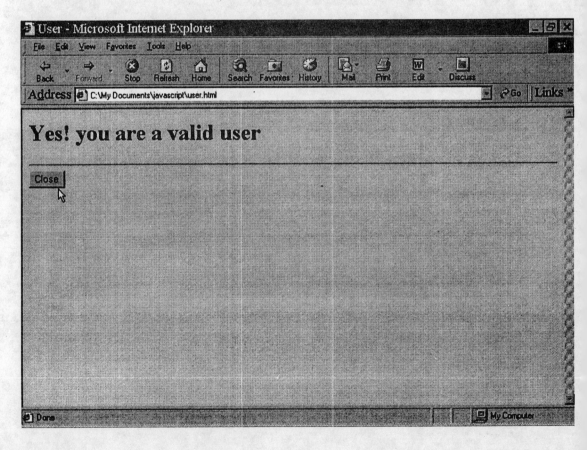

If the user types anything else then it shows a message in the same document. For example say the user had typed "computer" then it display the message Sorry! You are not a valid user – (user input)

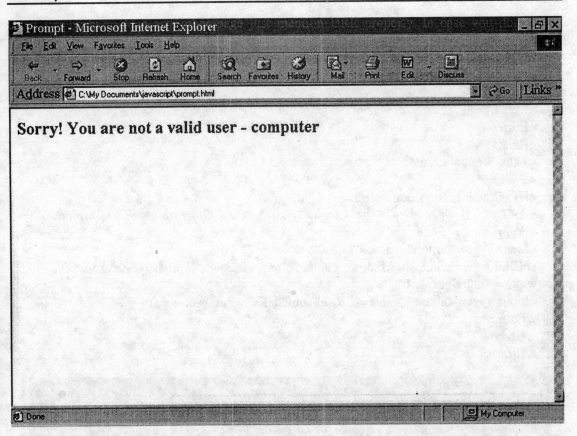

Creating a Window

Till now the window objects you have created are the dialog boxes like alert, confirm and prompt. Now lets create a window. The different components are as follows.

A variable is required to store the window object so that you can access the properties and methods of window object by using its name. For ex. newwindow is the variable name in this program.

```
<Input type="button" value="Open"
onClick="newwindow=window.open('c:','newwindow','toolbar=yes,
status=yes,width=300,height=250');">
```

After assigning a variable the next part is to load a window using window.open() which follows with the name of the URL. For ex.

```
<Input type="button" value="Open"
onClick="newwindow=window.open('c:','newwindow','toolbar=yes,status=yes,
width=300,height=250');">
```

In case you don't mention the URL your window appears blank. Here I have called C:, if you want to load any other page just mention URL properly. In case you don't want the toolbar or the status bar mention it as no.

```
<Input type="button" value="Open"
onClick="newwindow=window.open('c:','newwindow','toolbar=no,
status=no,width=300, height=250');">
```

Follow the code, which opens a window when the user clicks on the open button.

Code :

```
<Html>
<Head>
<Title>Window</Title>
<Body>
<H1>Creating A Window</H1>
<P>Click on Open to see the window and click on Close to close the window.</P>
<Form name="F1">
<Input type="button" value="Open"
onClick="newwindow=window.open('c:','newwindow','toolbar=yes,status=yes,
width=300,height=250');">
<Input type="button" value="Close" onClick="window.close()">
</Form>
</Body>
</Html>
```

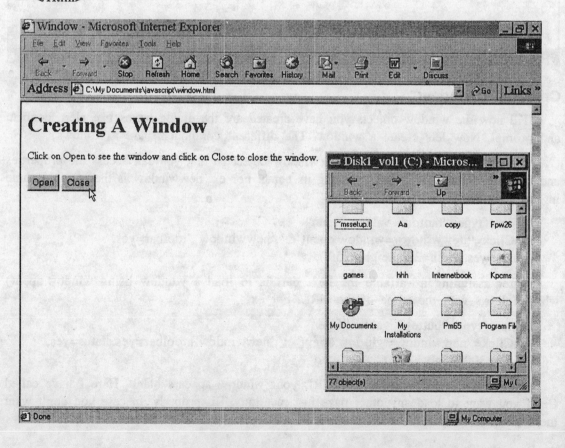

Working with Document Object

The HTML document contains various objects like images, hyperlinks, image maps, frames, forms etc. When the page gets loaded in the browser the browser creates an array for each HTML object and stores in the memory. You can say the browser registers each object and keeps a track of it. The array maintains an index, which helps in tracking each element individually. In case there is multiple object of similar type in the HTML document each array will have multiple indexed elements.

Working with Location Object

This window object stores information about the current URL (Uniform Resource Locator) stored in the window.

For ex. window.location.href=http//www.Microsoft.com; This statement will load this URL into the current window. The href property contains the URL of the window's current location. To access a portion of the URL you need to use various properties of Location Object for ex. Location protocol. Location object has two methods. They are as follows

location.reloads. This reloads the current document. It has the same function as Reload button of Netscape's toolbar.

location.replace. This replace the current location with the new location. You can replace manually also but it won't affect the browser's history. That means there is no effect of the back button.

Working with the History Object

History object stores the information about the visited URL's that has been visited before or after the current one. It also includes the method to move to the previous URLs or next URLs. History object does the similar function of array. Now lets see the properties of the history object.

history.length. This property keeps track of the visited locations number i.e. counting the number of location already visited by the user.

history.current. This property contains the value of the current visited location i.e. the URL of the page currently uploaded.

history.next. This property mentions the next URL in the history list. The user presses the forward button to move to the next URL if it is available.

history.previous. This property mentions the previous URL in the history list. The user presses the back button to move to the previous URL.

It has three methods

history.go. Opens a URL available in the history list. To use this method you have to specify the positive or negative number in parentheses. That means +2 is equal to pressing the forward button twice.

history.back. This method loads the previous URL in the history list. That means pressing the back button once.

history.forward. This method loads the next URL in the history list if available i.e. the current page should not be the last URL. It is equivalent of pressing the forward button once.

Follow the code, which shows the function of history objects. In this example you will find two icons (Previous and Forward), which function like previous and forward buttons uses these methods to navigate the browser. You can replace the icons with simple text. For testing the code visit other URLs and then try the previous and forward buttons.

Code :

```
<Html>
<Head>
<Title>Using History Objects</Title>
</Head>
<Body>
<H1>Working with History Objects</H1>
<hr>
<Font size=4>
<P>Lets navigate between the browser using the History Objects. Click on the previous
and forward icons.</P>
<A href="JavaScript:history.go(-1);"><Img src="C:\Program Files\Microsoft Visual
Studio\Common\Graphics\Icons\Arrows\Point02.ico" border="0"></A>
<A href="JavaScript:history.go(1);"><Img src="C:\Program Files\Microsoft Visual
Studio\Common\Graphics\Icons\Arrows\Point04.ico" border="0"></A>
</Body>
</Html>.
```

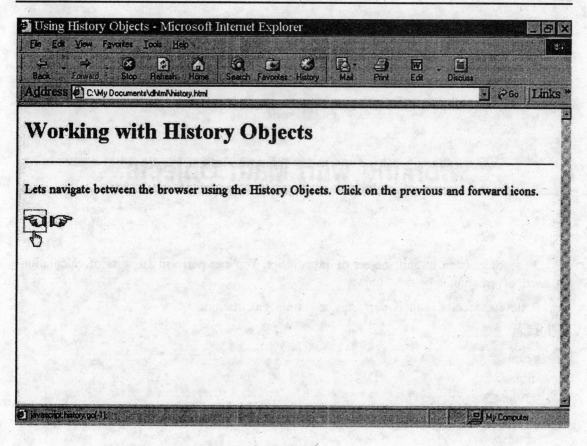

** ** **

19

Working with Math Objects

This object is an in-built object of Java Script. You can perform all sorts of calculations no need of creating any new object.

Follow the code, which performs a simple calculation.

Code :

```
<Html>
<Head>
<Title>Calculation</Title>
</Head>
<Body>
<Form name=f1>
<Script Language="JavaScript">
function calc(form)
{
   f1.total.value=eval(f1.eng.value)+eval(f1.maths.value)+eval(f1.computer.value);
   f1.average.value=eval(f1.total.value)/3;
}
</Script>
<center><H1>Calculation</H1></center><Br><Br>
<Font size=4>
<P>
```

Enter the marks obtained by you in English,Maths and Computer and then click on calculate button. It will calculate the Total marks and the Average marks.<P>
Enter your English Marks:

```
<Input type="text" name="eng" Value="" size=3><Br><Br>
```

Enter your Maths Marks:

```
<Input type="text" name="maths" Value="" size=3><Br><Br>
```

Enter your Computer Marks:

```
<Input type="text" name="computer" Value="" size=3><Br><Br>
<Input type="button" Value="Calculate" onClick="calc(this.f1);"><Br>
<Br>
Total Marks :
<Input type="text" Name="total" size=4 onFocus="this.blur();">
Average Marks :
<Input type="text" Name="average" size=4 onFocus="this.blur();">
</Form>
</Body>
</Html>
```

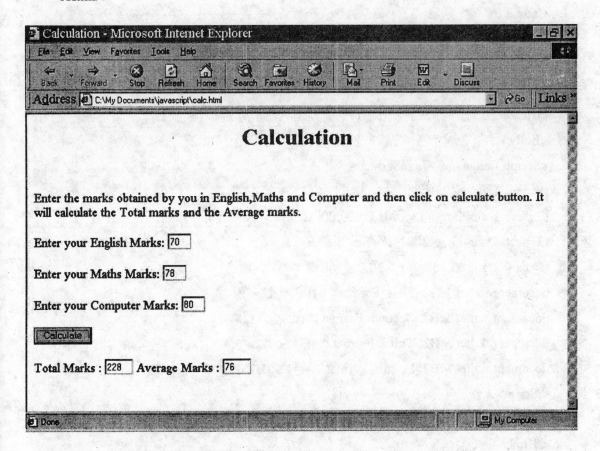

There are three different methods of Math object, which allows you to round or truncate decimal values. For ex. instead of writing 5.333 write 5.32. So like this

Math.ceil(). It rounds the number to its next integer, i.e. 6.767 to 6.8.

Math.floor(). It rounds the number down to its next integer, i.e. 6.767 to 6.6.

Math.round(). It rounds the number to its nearest integer, i.e. 6.767 to 6.7.

Working with Date Object

Date object too is an in-built object of Java Script. Mainly used to handle dates and time efficiently. Date object has no properties. You can create the date object by using the new keyword. Note the following date format.

Holiday = new Date(); - It will store the current date.

Holiday = new Date("May 15,2001,06:30:00");

Holiday = new Date(05,15,2001);

Holiday = new Date(05,20,2001,06,30,0);

Follow the example, which displays the date in different formats. Note the difference in the browser view.

Code :

```
<Html>
<Head>
<Title>Date</Title>
</Head>
<Body>
<Script Language="JavaScript">
t1=new Date()+"<Br>";
t2=new Date("May 15,2001,06:30:00")+"<Br>";
t3=new Date(05,15,2001)+"<Br>";
t4=new Date(05,15,2001,6,30,0)+"<Br>";
document.write("<H2>First Format "+t1+"</H2>");
document.write("<H2>Second Format "+t2+"</H2>");
document.write("<H2>Third Format "+t3+"</H2>");
document.write("<H2>Fourth Format "+t4+"</H2>");
</Script>
</Body>
</Html>
```

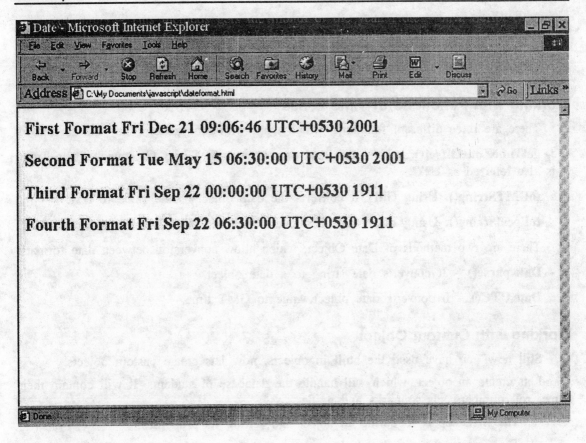

Set methods

You can set the components of the date object using set methods. The different set methods are as follows.

SetDate() – This method sets the day of the month.

SetMonth() – This methods sets the month of the year. Note – Java Script calculates month numbers from 0 to 11 so 0 is January and December is 11.

SetFullYear() – Sets the year.

Set Time() – Sets the time and the date.

SetHours(), SetMinutes() and SetSeconds() sets the time.

Get methods

Now to get the values from the Date object you have to use get method. The different get methods are as follows.

getDate() – This method gets the day of the month.

getMonth() – This methods gets the month of the year. Note – Java Script calculates month numbers from 0 to 11 so 0 is January and December is 11.

getFullYear() – gets the year.

get Time() – gets the time and the date.

getHours(), getMinutes() and getSeconds() gets the time.

Working with Functions of Time zones

There are three different functions, which work with time zones. They are as follows

getTimeZoneOffset(). It gives the local time zone of GMT i.e. Greenwich Mean Time. It is also referred as UTC.

toGMTString(). Using GMT it converts the date object's time value to text.

toLocalString(). Using Local time it converts the date object's time value to text.

There are two methods of Date Object, which allow conversion between date formats.

Date.parse() – It converts date string to a date object.

Date.UTC() – It converts date object value to GMT time.

Working with Custom Object

Still now you have used the built in objects, now lets create custom objects.

Lets create an object, which will handle the database of students. It will contain their name, roll.numbers, class, marks and grade.

⇨ The first step is to define an object and setting its properties.

⇨ Then create a function, which works as constructor of an object. The constructor accepts the parameters for initializing the object and then assigns them to the corresponding properties of the object. The keyword "this" is used for creating objects definition.

For example

```
function information(name,address,phone,email)
{
   this.name=name;
   this.address=address;
   this.phone=phone;
   this.email=email;
}
```

⇨ In this example mentioned above the function name given as information, so the object is information object. Then define the object method by calling a function and then assigns them as properties of the object.

⇨ The function reads the properties from this object and is displayed. While displaying you can skip a line for better display performance.

⇨ Then the last part is to create a new object using the new keyword for using the object definition i.e. creating the object instance.

Now follow the code, which displays the data of various students by the use of custom objects.

```
<Html>
<Head>
<Title>Creating custom objects</Title>
<Script Language="JavaScript">
function students()
{
    name="<I>Name :</I>"+this.name+"<Br>";
    roll="<I>Roll Numbers :</I>"+this.roll+"<Br>";
    marks="<I>Marks :</I>"+this.marks+"<Br>";
    grade="<I>Grade :</I>"+this.grade+"<Br>";
    document.write(name,roll,marks,grade);
    document.write("<hr color=red>");
}
function stud(n,r,c,m,g)
{
    this.name=n;
    this.roll=r;
    this.marks=m;
    this.grade=g;
    this.students=students;
}
</Script>
</Head>
<Body>
<H1>Creating Custom Objects</H1>
<Script Language="JavaScript">
sudha=new stud("Sudha Dasgupta","A001","X","67%","B");
rina=new stud("Rina Mallick","A002","XI","86%","A");
mina=new stud("Mina Bhatnagar","A003","X","78%","B");
sudha.students();
rina.students();
mina.students();
</Script>
</Body>
</Html>
```

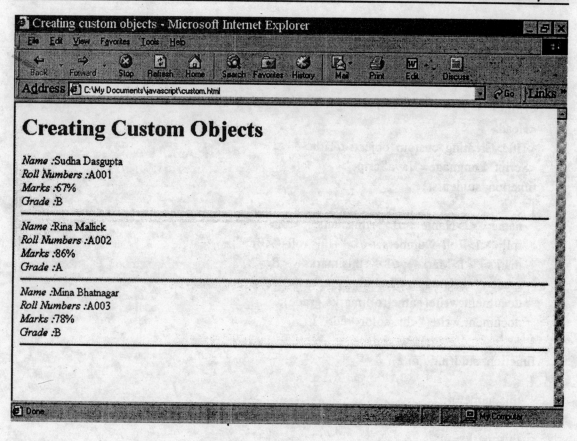

20
Working with Scrolling Message

When you browse the net you find message scrolling down in the status bar. This you can create using Java Script.

First you have set the message in a variable. Then add another variable just to allocate some space. This is necessary to show the end of the message. Then you need a variable to set the starting point, which will store the current position of the string. The scrolling is done by the use of scrollingMsg function.

Now follow the code, which displays the scrolling message

Code :

```
<Html>
<Head>
<Title>Scrolling Message</Title>
<Script Language="JavaScript">
Msg="Click on the subject you want to learn.";
Space="           ";
Start=10;
function scrollingMsg()
{
    window.status=Msg.substring(Start,Msg.length)+Space+Msg.substring(0,Start);
    Start++;
    if(Start>Msg.length) Start=0;
    window.setTimeout("scrollingMsg()",250);
}
scrollingMsg();
</Script>
</Head>
<Body>
```

```
<Center><H1>Online Training</H1></Center>
<P>Online Training helps you to train yourself at your own time. So join us today and welcome a bright future.</P>
<A Href="C:\My Documents\javascript\C++.html">C++</A><Br>
<A Href="C:\My Documents\javascript\Visual Java.html">Visual Java</A><Br>
<A Href="C:\My Documents\javascript\Visual Basic.html">Visual Basic</A><Br>
<A Href="C:\My Documents\javascript\Visual C++.html">Visual C++</A><Br>
</Body>
</Html>
```

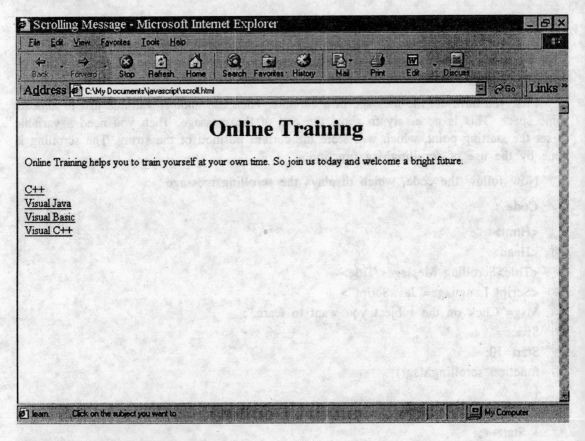

Working with Link Descriptions

Link Descriptions will show a description of the link in the status line. This is a common feature of the event handler.

Follow the code, which displays Link Descriptions

Code :

```
<Html>
<Head>
<Title>Descriptions</Title>
<Script language="JavaScript">
function dinner(text)
{
   window.status = text;
   return true;
}
function clear()
{
   window.status=" ";
}
</Script>
</Head>
<Body>
<H2>Dinner Club</H2>
<P>Hold the mouse over the link to see the description of the web page.</P>
<Ol>
<Li><A Href="C:\My Documents\javascript\Soup.html" onMouseOver="dinner('Shows
the list of available Soup dishes'); return true;" onMouseOut="clear();">Soup dishes </
A>
<Li><A Href="C:\My Documents\javascript\Chinese.html"
onMouseOver="dinner('Shows the list of available Chinese dishes'); return true;"
onMouseOut="clear();">Chinese dishes </A>
<Li><A Href="C:\My Documents\javascript\Moghlai.html"
onMouseOver="dinner('Shows the list of available Moghlai dishes'); return true;"
onMouseOut="clear();">Moghlai dishes </A>
<Li><A Href="C:\My Documents\javascript\Indian.html" onMouseOver="dinner('Shows
the list of available Indian dishes'); return true;" onMouseOut="clear();">Indian dishes
</A>
</Ol>
</Body>
</Html>
```

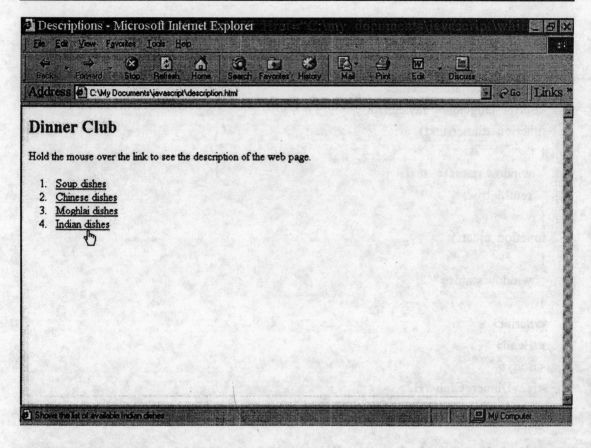

Image Map

Now a day's Image Maps are quite popular. The image is divided into different areas or regions using Area Coords. According to your requirement you can set messages in those locations. When the user clicks on any location of the image a connection is made with an URL, which appears.

Follow the code, which shows Image Map handling

Code :

```
<Html>
<Head>
<Title>Image map</Title>
</Head>
<Body>
<H1>Working with Image Map</H1>
<Img src="C:\My Documents\webdesign\flower4.jpg"   USEMAP="#flower">
<Map Name="flower">
<Area Coords="80,88,208,125" Href="C:\my documents\javascript\while.html"
onMouseOver="window.status='Pink Rose'; return true;">
```

```
<Area Coords="80,84,208,125" Href="C:\my documents\javascript\while.html"
onMouseOver="window.status='Yellow Rose'; return true;">
<Area Coords="70,88,208,125" Href="C:\my documents\javascript\while.html"
onMouseOver="window.status='Red Rose'; return true;">
</Map>
</Body>
<Html>
```

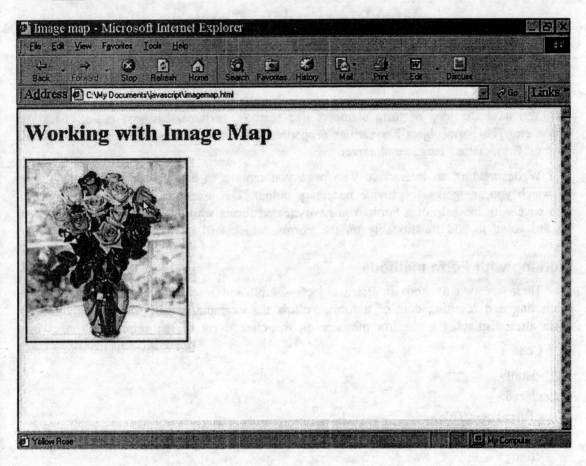

❋ ❋ ❋

21

Working with Forms

You have the idea of form elements like textbox, textarea, Listbox, radio, checkbox, button etc. The Form object has various properties like action, encoding, method (it includes Post or Get), name, length and target.

While creating an interactive web page you require to capture the users input based on which you are going to provide necessary output. The users input is collected from the web page with the help of a Form. You have created forms while working with HTML. Now we are going to add functionality on the Forms, which will interact with the user.

Working with Form methods

There are two methods in Form objects submit and reset. They are mainly used for submitting and resetting data of a form. Follow the example, which submits data from a Form after displaying a confirm message on the click event of the submit button.

Code :

```
<Html>
<Head>
<Title>Vote</Title>
</Head>
<Body>
<Form>
<Script Language="JavaScript">
function Sub()
{
   confirm("Thankyou! for participating in the vote");
}
</Script>
<Font size=4>
```

<P>Vote your Favourite Cricketer and if you are lucky you can free tickets for the test match.</P>
<Input type="Radio" name="r1"="on">Rahul Dravid
<Input type="Radio" name="r1"="on">Sachin Tendulkar
<Input type="Radio" name="r1"="on">Ajit Agerkar
<Input type="Radio" name="r1"="on">Saurav Ganguly
<hr>
<Center>
<H2>Enter your Details:</H2></Center>
First Name: <Input type="text" Name="Firstname" size=20>
Last Name: <Input type="text" Name="Lastname" size=20><P>
Address: <Input type="text" Name="Address" size=60><P>
Pincode: <Input type="text" Name="Pincode" size=6><P>
E-mail: <Input type="text" Name="email" id="email" size=20><P>
<Input type="Submit" Value="Submit" onClick='Sub()'>
</Form>
</Body>
</Html

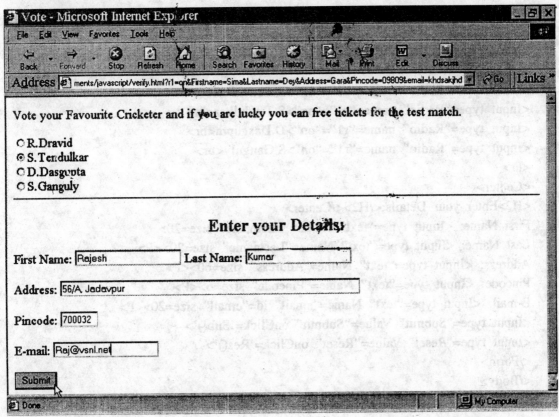

Now in the same Form lets add a reset button, which will reset the data of the Form after displaying an alert message.

Code :

```
<Html>
<Head>
<Title>Vote</Title>
</Head>
<Body>
<Form>
<Script Language="JavaScript">
function Sub()
{
   confirm("Thankyou! for participating in the vote");
}
function Res()
{
   alert("All the data of the form will be cleared");
}
</Script>
<Font size=4>
<P>Vote your Favourite Cricketer and if you are lucky you can free tickets for the test match.</P>
<Input type="Radio" name="r1"="on">R.Dravid<br>
<Input type="Radio" name="r1"="on">S.Tendulkar<br>
<Input type="Radio" name="r1"="on">D.Dasgupta<br>
<Input type="Radio" name="r1"="on">S.Ganguly<br>
<hr>
<Center>
<H2>Enter your Details:</H2></Center>
First Name: <Input type="text" Name="Firstname" size=20>
Last Name: <Input type="text" Name="Lastname" size=20><P>
Address: <Input type="text" Name="Address" size=60><P>
Pincode: <Input type="text" Name="Pincode" size=6><P>
E-mail: <Input type="text" Name="email" id="email" size=20><P>
<Input type="Submit" Value="Submit" onClick='Sub()'>
<Input type="Reset" Value="Reset" onClick='Res()'>
</Form>
</Body>
</Html>
```

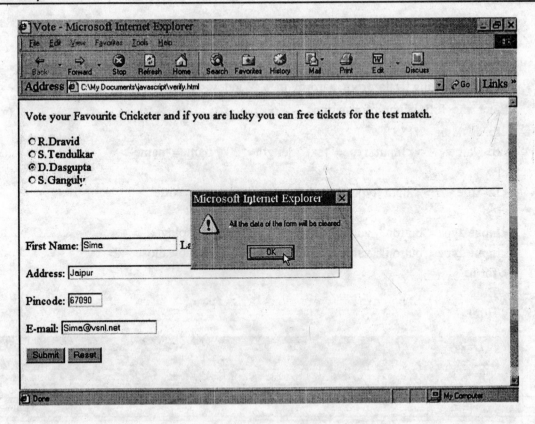

So when the user clicks on OK of the alert message all fields get cleared.

Event Handlers of Form object

onSubmit and onReset are the two event handlers of a form object. You can perform work based on these handlers. For ex. Calling a function within the <Form> tag.

Displaying Data

This program displays the name in a window from a Form. A function is created which creates the window and displays the data in it. Follow the code to find it out.

```
<Html>
<Head>
<Title>Form Example</Title>
<Script Language="JavaScript">
function display()
{
   win=window.open('','Newwin','toolbar=yes,status=yes,width=300,height=150')
   msg="<B>Hello you are Mr/Mrs </B>" +document.f1.name.value+"
   "+document.f1.title.value;
   win.document.write(msg);
}
```

```
</Script>
</Head>
<Body>
<H1>Displaying Data from a form in a Window</H1>
Enter the following information.
<form name="f1">
<B>Name:</B><Input type="text" length="20" name="name">
<P>
<B>Title:</B><Input type="text" length="30" name="title">
<P>
<Input type="button" value="Display" onClick="display();">
<Input type="button" value="Close" onClick="window.close();">
</form>
</Body>
</Html>
```

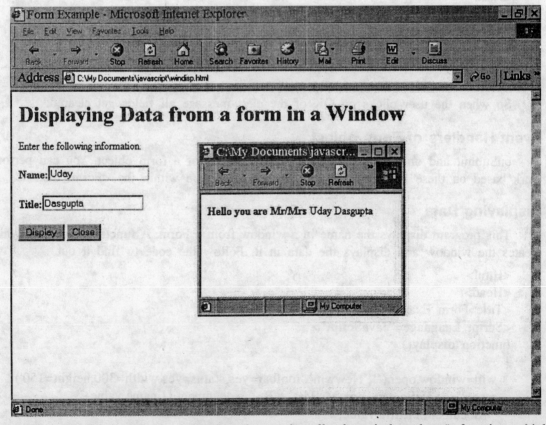

When the user clicks on the close button it calls the window.close() function which displays a confirm dialog. Click yes to close the window.

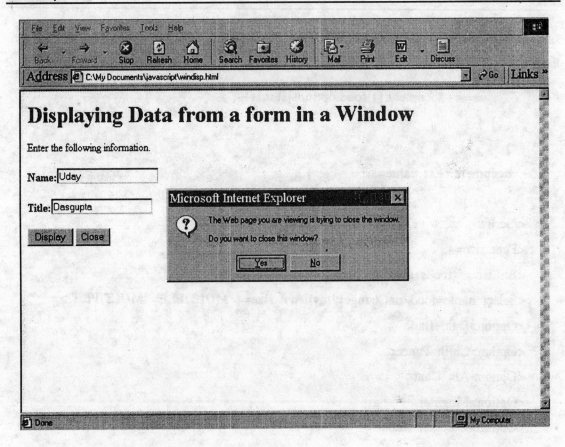

Working with Multi Choice Select List

To work with multiple choices you have to add <MULTIPLE> attribute in the select object. This will help you in multi selection. Now follow the code, which adds the items name in the text box due to multi selection.

Code :

```
<Html>
<Body background="C:\Program Files\Common Files\Microsoft
Shared\Stationery\Sunflower Bkgrd.jpg">
<Form name=f1>
<Script Language="JavaScript">
function mylist()
{
    var sr="";
    n=document.f1.food.length;
    for(i=0;i<n;++i)
```

```
      {
         if(document.f1.food.options[i].selected)
         {
            sr=sr+document.f1.food.options[i].text+",";
         }
      }
      document.f1.t1.value=sr;
}
</Script>
<Font size=4>
<B>List of foods available<br><br>
<Select name=food onChange='mylist()' size=4 MULTIPLE="MULTIPLE">
<Option>Dahi Bada
<Option>Chilli Paneer
<Option>Alu Chat
<Option>Moghlai
<Option>Chicken Kabab
<Option>Sahe Paneer
</Select>
<P>
The order is placed for
<Input type=Text name=t1 size=40></P>
<P></B>
Enter your Address<Input type="Text" name=t2 size=50>
Pin<Input type="Text" name=t3 size=10><Br></P>
<P>Nearest Location<Input type="Text" name=t4 size=40><Br></P>
<Input type="Submit" name=b1 value="Click! To place the Order.">
</Form>
</Body>
</Html>
```

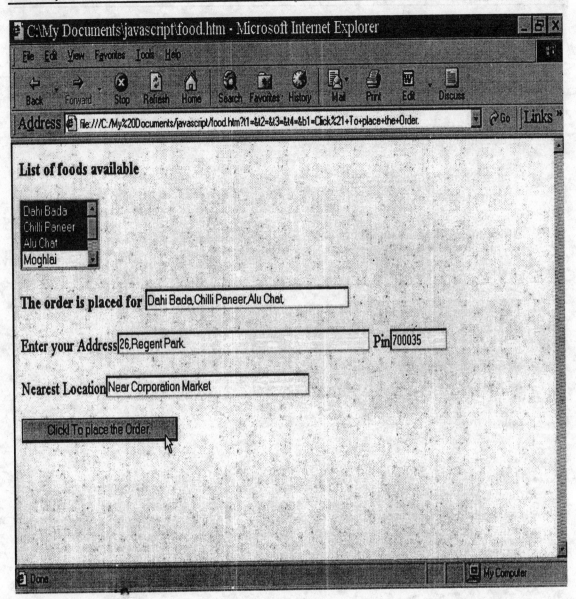

Validating a Form

Sometimes wrong data, incomplete data hampers the work so to control, validation is required. You have to create validation according to your requirement. You also have to give proper information against validation. For example – If the user is leaving a field bank and due to validation the user cannot submit, then it is necessary to display a message for guiding the user. Follow the example, which restricts blank entry.

```
<Html>
<Head>
<Title>Validating Form</Title>
<Script Language="JavaScript">
function validation()
{
  if(document.f1.name.value.length<1)
  {
    alert("Enter your name");
    return false;
  }
  if(document.f1.roll.value.length<2)
  {
    alert("Enter your Roll No.");
    return false;
  }
  if(document.f1.email.value.length<1)
  {
  alert("Enter your E-mail");
  return false;
  }
  return true;
}
</Script>
</Head>
<Body Bgcolor="yellow">
<H1>Validating a Form</H1>
Fill the details properly and then click on submit button to enroll your name in our
program.
<Form name="f1" onSubmit=validation()>
<P>
<B><I>Name: <Input type="text" length="20" name="name">
<P>
<B><I>Roll no: <Input type="text" length="20" name="roll">
<P>
<B><I>E-mail: <Input type="text" length="20" name="email">
<P>
<Input type="Submit" Value="Finish">
</Form>
</Body>
</Html>
```

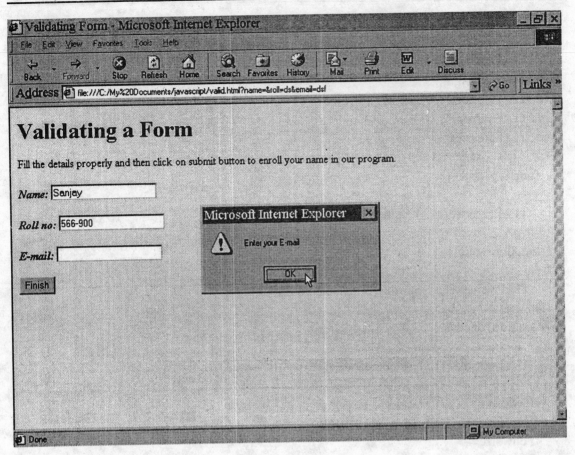

Handling Data in Form

Follow the example, which adds text from the textbox to Listbox. After writing the text user had to click the Add button to add the text in the Listbox. The Form contains Delete button, which deletes the data from the Listbox, and the edit button edits the data of the list. For editing select the text from the list, it appears in the textbox, after editing the user had to click on Edit.

Code :

```
<Html>
<Head>
<Title>Working with Form</Title>
</Head>
<Body>
<Script Language="JavaScript">
var fso;
function onadd()
```

```
{
    var l,a=0;
    f1.s1.add(document.createElement('<option>'));
    l=f1.s1.length;
    f1.s1.options[l-1].text=f1.t1.value;
    f1.t1.value='';
    f1.t1.focus();
}
function ondel()
{
    f1.s1.remove(f1.s1.SelectedIndex);
}
function selto()
{
    f1.t1.value=f1.s1.options[f1.s1.selectedIndex].text;
}
function oned()
{
    f1.s1.options[f1.s1.selectedIndex].text=f1.t1.value;
}
</Script>
<H1>Handling Data in a Form</H1>
<Font size=4>
<P>
```

The add button adds the text of the textbox in the list. Delete button allows you to delete the text from the listbox.The edit buttons replace the text after editing.</P>

```
<Form name=f1 id=f1>
Enter your name :<Input type=text name=t1 id=t1>
<Br>
List of Names :
<Br>
<Select id=s1 name=s1 size=4 onchange='selto()'></Select>
<P>
<Input type="button" value="Add" onClick='onadd()'>
<Input type="button" value="Del" onClick='ondel()'>
<Input type="button" value="Edit" onClick='oned()'>
</P>
</Form>
</body>
</Html>
```

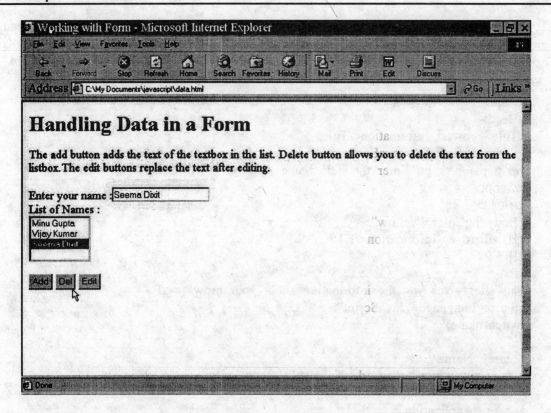

In this example the Add buttons adds the data in the list box. The Delete button deletes the text from the list after selecting it from the list box. The Edit buttons edits the text. The text appears in the text box once it is selected from the list. After editing the user have to click the edit button, which replace the old text with the edited text.

Getting the Browser Information

To get the information about the Browser you can use the navigator object.

The different properties are as follows.

Navigator.appCodeName. Shows the internal code of the Browser. For ex. Mozilla

Navigator.appName. Shows the Browser's name currently you are using. For ex. Microsoft Internet Explorer

Navigator.appVersion. Shows the version of the Browser currently you are using. For ex. 4.0 (compatible; MSIE 5.01; Windows 98)

Navigator.userAgent. Shows the userAgent. It's the string, which the browser sends while requesting for a page. For example Mozilla/4.0 (compatible; MSIE 5.01; Windows 98)

Navigator.language. Shows the language your browser is using. It shows in letter code. For ex. en for English.

Navigator.platform. Shows the platform of the browser. For ex. Win32.

Follow the code where the prompt appears when you load the page. Type the item you want to know about (For ex. to know about the version type Version and then click OK. Then it will show the version of your browser currently you are using).

Code :

```html
<Html>
<Head>
<Title>Browser Information</Title>
<Script Language="JavaScript">
var name=prompt("Enter the item name to view the information","name");
</Script>
</Head>
<Body bgColor="yellow">
<H1>Browser Information</H1>
<Hr>
<P>
This sites gives you the information about your browser.</P>
<Script Language="JavaScript">
switch(name)
{
    case "Name":
    document.write("<B>Code Name:</B>"+navigator.appCodeName);
    break;
    case "Application":
    document.write("<B>Code App Name:</B>"+navigator.appName);
    break;
    case "Version":
    document.write("<B>Code App Version:</B>"+navigator.appVersion);
    break;
    case "User Agent":
    document.write("<B>Code User Agent:</B>"+navigator.userAgent);
    break;
    case "Language":
    document.write("<B>Code Language:</B>"+navigator.language);
    break;
    case "Platform":
    document.write("<B>Code Platform:</B>"+navigator.platform);
    break;
    default:
    window.alert("Entered a wrong item");
    break;
}
</Script>
<Hr>
</Body>
</Html>
```

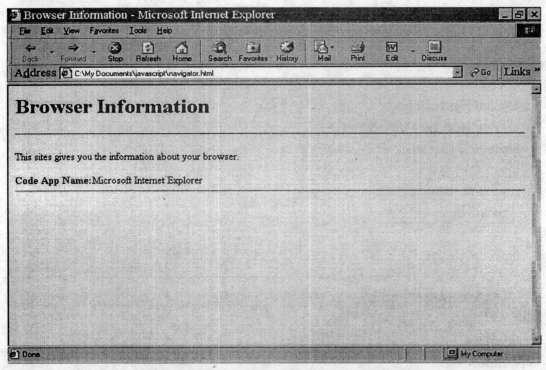

Browser view in Microsoft Internet Explorer

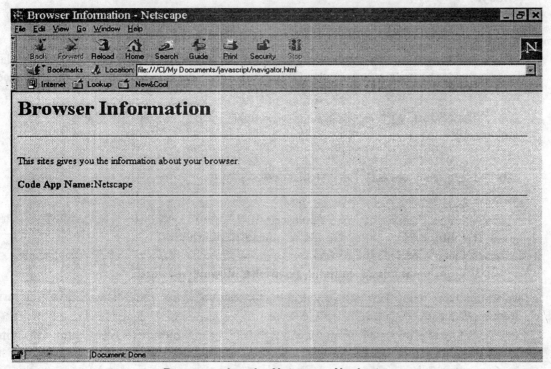

Browser view in Netscape Navigator

PROJECT

Code of Project1.html :

```
<Html>
<Head>
<Title>Project</Title>
<Script language="JavaScript">
function edu(text)
{
    window.status = text;
    return true;
}
function clear()
{
    window.status=" ";
}
</Script>
</Head>
<Body>
<Center><H1>Online Education</H1></Center>
<Font size=4>
```

<P>Online Education the famous organisation has announced different courses for the students to build their career in the IT industry. The students have to pass the entrance test to join the course.

The entrance test will be held on 2nd January. The last date of admission is 31st January.</P>

```
<Hr>
```

<P>The avaialble courses are listed below:</P>

```
<Ul>
<Li><A href="C:\my documents\javascript\BCA.html" onMouseOver="edu('This site
gives the information about the BCA course'); return true;"
onMouseOut="clear();">BCA</A>
<Li><A href="c:\my documents\javascript\MCA.html"
onMouseOver="edu('This site gives the information about the MCA course'); return
true;" onMouseOut="clear();">MCA</A>
<Li><A href="c:\my documents\javascript\BSC.html" onMouseOver="edu('This site
gives the information about the BSC course'); return true;" onMouseOut="clear();">Bsc
in Computer Science</A>
```

```
<Li><A href="C:\my documents\javascript\BBA.html" onMouseOver="edu('This site
gives the information about the BBA course'); return true;"
onMouseOut="Clear();">BBA</A>

<Li><A href="C:\my documents\javascript\MBA.html" onMouseOver="edu('This site
gives the information about the MBA course'); return true;"
onMouseOut="Clear();">MBA</A>

</Ul>
</Body>
</Html>
```

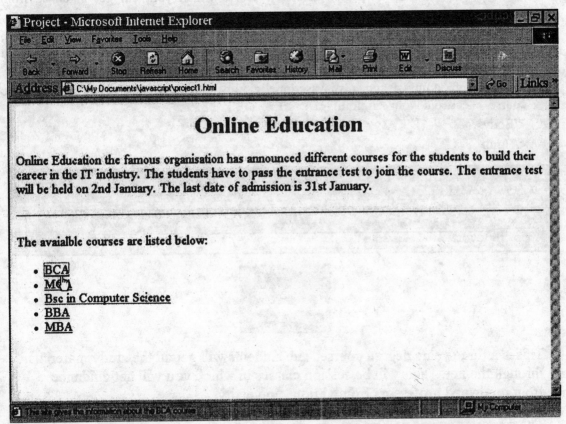

Code for BCA.html:

```
<Html>
<Head>
<Title>BCA</Title>
</Head>
<Body>
<Script Language="JavaScript">
function msg()
```

```
{
    alert("If you pass our eligibility test you can join the course");
}
</Script>
<Center><img src="C:\my documents\bca.bmp"></center>
<Font size="5">
<P>
```

This is a three years degree course. The students will get all the study materials through the net. Their will be session classes in which you will get guidance from renowned professors from various university.<P>

<P>The semester exams will be held on every six months interval. Exams syllabus, date and other information will be mailed to the students two months before the exams.</P>

<P><A href="c:\my documents\javascript\eligibility.html" onClick="msg()">To join the course check out your eligibility</A></P>

```
</Body>
</Html>
```

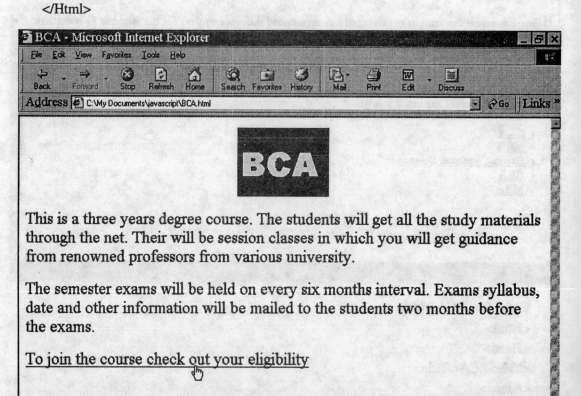

When the user clicks on the link an alert message appears.

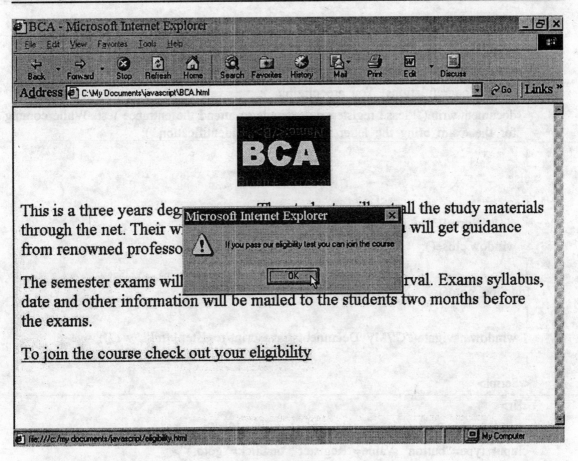

Now the users have to click the OK button and the prompt appears when the eligibility.html gets uploaded.

Code for eligibility.html :

```
<Html>
<Head>
<Title>Eligibility Test</Title>
<Script language="JavaScript">
var tot=prompt("Enter your total marks of science group in Higher Secondary","tot");
</Script>
</Head>
<Body>
<center><H1>Eligibility Test</H1></center><Br><Br>
<Font size=5>
```

```
<Script language="JavaScript">
if(tot>200)
{
    alert("Congratulations! You are eligible");
    document.write("Please register your details to attend the entrance test. While coming
    for the exam bring the letter sent by us for identification.");
}
else
{
    alert("Sorry! You are not eligible");
    window.close();
}
function goto()
{
    window.navigate("C:/My Documents/javascript/register.html","w1");
}
</Script>
<Hr>
<P>Click the Register button to register yourself.</P>
<Input type="button" Value="Register" onClick="goto()">
</Body>
</Html>
```

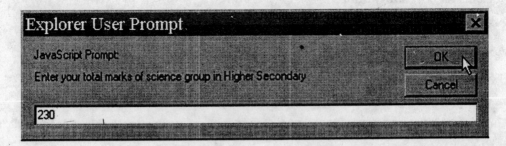

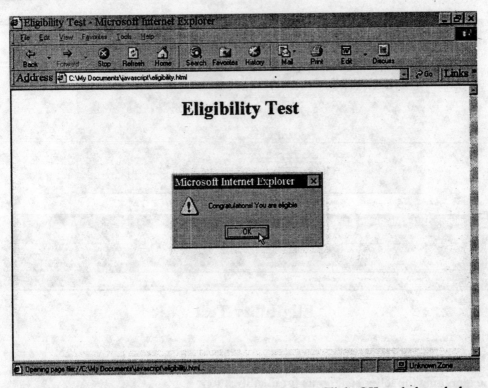

This alert message appears if the condition satisfies. Click OK and the whole page get loaded. But if the condition fails it displays an alert message conveying sorry for the users.

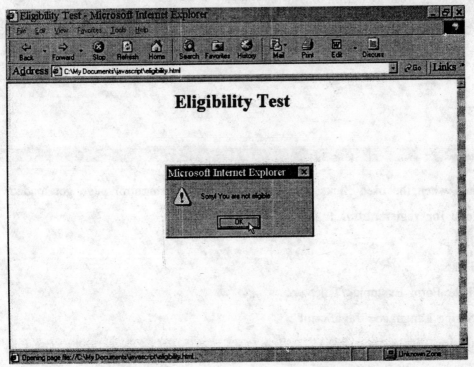

When the user clicks OK of the alert message then the window closure message appears and the user gets terminated from the page by clicking the Yes button.

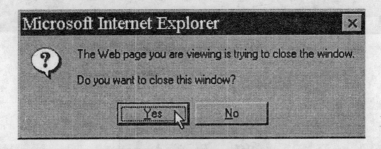

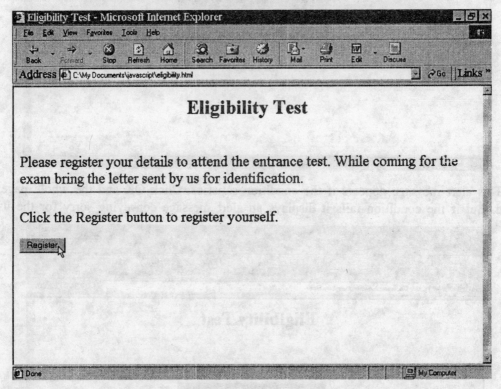

Here when the user clicks on Register button, register.html page get loaded.

Code for register.html :

```
<Html>
<Head>
<Title>Form Example</Title>
<Script Language="JavaScript">
function display()
```

```
{
    win=window.open('','Newwin','toolbar=yes,status=yes,width=300,height=150')
    msg="<Ul><Li><B>Name:</B>" +document.f1.name.value;
    msg+="<Li><B>Address:</B>"+document.f1.address.value;
    msg+="<Li><B>City:</B>"+document.f1.city.value;
    msg+="<Li><B>Phone:</B>"+document.f1.phone.value;
    msg+="<Li><B>E-mail:</B>"+document.f1.email.value+"</Ul>";
    msg+="<B>Your registration has been confirmed.</B>";
    win.document.write(msg);
}
function home()
{
    window.navigate("C:/My Documents/javascript/project1.html","w1");
}
</Script>
</Head>
<Body>
<H1>Registration Form</H1>
<Hr>
<Font size="4">
<P>Enter the following information and confirm your registration. After you finish
click on Register button.</P>
<form name="f1">
<B>Name:</B><Input type="text" length="20" name="name">
<P>
<B>Address:</B><Input type="text" length="30" name="address">
<P>
<B>City:</B><Input type="text" length="15" name="city">
<P>
<B>Phone:</B><Input type="text" length="10" name="phone">
<P>
<B>E-mail:</B><Input type="text" length="20" name="email">
<P>
<Input type="button" value="Register" onClick="display();">
<Input type="button" value="Return" onClick="home();">
<Input type="button" value="Close" onClick="window.close();">
</form>
</Body>
</Html>
```

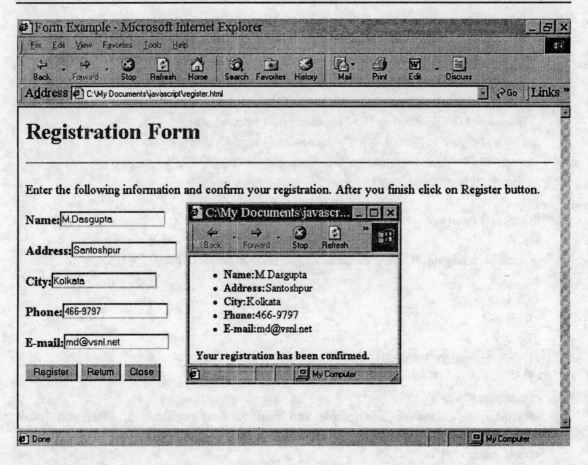

After giving all the information when the user clicks on Register button the confirmation of Registration message appears inside a window with all the details given by the user. This page contains another two buttons. The Return buttons opens the starting page i.e. the project1.html page and close button closes the window.

Assignments

The example shows the registration details for BCA course, now you try for the other subjects i.e. for MCA, BSC, BBA, and MBA and then create the link to join them with this project.

❅ ❅ ❅

22

Working with JSSS

Lets create style sheets using JSSS objects. The three main objects that JSSS handles are Tags, Classes and ids.

Now follow this code which is written using CSS i.e. Cascading Style Sheet.

Code :

```
<Html>
<Head>
<Title>Text Formatting</Title>
</Head>
<Style>
Body {Background: pink;
color: blue; margin - left: 0.5in;
margin - right: 0.5in}
H1 {font-size:26; font-family:Monotype Corsiva; color: red;}
H2 {font-size:24; color: yellow; font-weight:bold; background: red}
P {Font-size:18pt; font style: Italic;}
</Style>
<Body>
<Center><H1>Internet</H1></Center>
<P>Internet connection is now available at Rs.1000 for 100 hrs. For 50 hrs we are
charging Rs.500 and for 25 hrs Rs.250.<P>
<Center><H2>Diwali Offer</H2></Center>
<P>50 hrs free connection with 100 hrs connection. 20 hrs free with 50 hrs connection
and 10 hrs free with 25 hrs connection.
</p>
</Body>
</Html>
```

Now the same program is written again using JSSS i.e. Java Script Style Sheet. Note the difference between the scripting tags.

```
<Html>
<Head>
<Title>Text Formatting using JSSS</Title>
</Head>
<Style type="text/javascript">
with(tags.Body)
{
   backgroundColor="pink";
   color="blue";
   marginLeft="50";
   marginRight="50";
}
with(tags.H1)
{
   fontSize="26pt";
   fontFamily="Monotype Corsiva";
   color="red";
}
with(tags.H2)
{
   fontSize="24pt";
   fontWeight="bold";
   backgroundColor="red";
   color="yellow";
}
   with(tags.P)
{
   fontSize="18pt";
   fontStyle="Italic";
}
</Style>
<Body>
<Center><H1>Internet</H1></Center>
<P>Internet connection is now available at Rs.1000 for 100 hrs.
For 50 hrs we are charging Rs.500 and for 25 hrs Rs.250.<P>
```

```
<Center><H2>Diwali Offer</H2></Center>
<P>50 hrs free connection with 100 hrs connection.
20 hrs free with 50 hrs connection and 10 hrs free with 25 hrs connection.
</p>
</Body>
</Html>
```

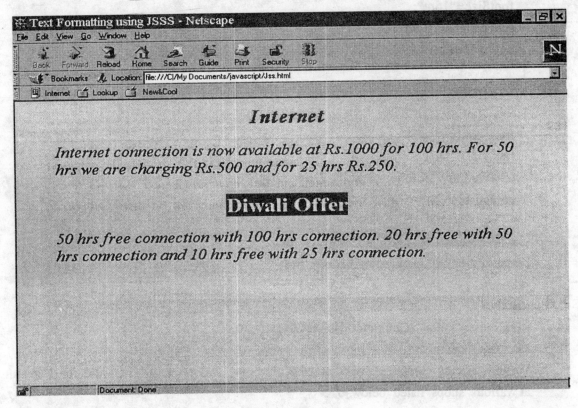

Working with Class object of JSSS

Follow the code where classes have been used to make the page more dynamic.

```
<Html>
<Head> .
<Title>Adding Class</Title>
</Head>
<Style type="text/javascript">
with(tags.Body)
{
    backgroundColor="lightgreen";
    marginLeft=".60";
```

```
        marginRight=".60";
        marginTop=".15";
    }
    with(tags.P)
    {
        fontFamily="garamond";
        fontSize="16pt";
        fontWeight="Bold";
        color="red";
    }
    with(tags.Ol)
    {
        fontFamily="Arial";
        fontSize="18pt";
        fontWeight="Bold"
        color="blue";
    }
    classes.color.all.backgroundColor="yellow";
    classes.color1.all.backgroundColor="lime";
</Style>
<Body>
<H1 class="color">Computer Books</H1>
<P class="color1">
We are offering computer books at 15% discount. This offer will be valid for 1 month
at various shops listed below.</P>
<Ol>
<Li>Computer Books Store
<Li>All about Computers
<Li>Computer Knowledge
</Ol>
<P class="color">The shops are open from morning 10 a.m to 7 p.m. Sunday closed
</P>
</Body>
</Html>
```

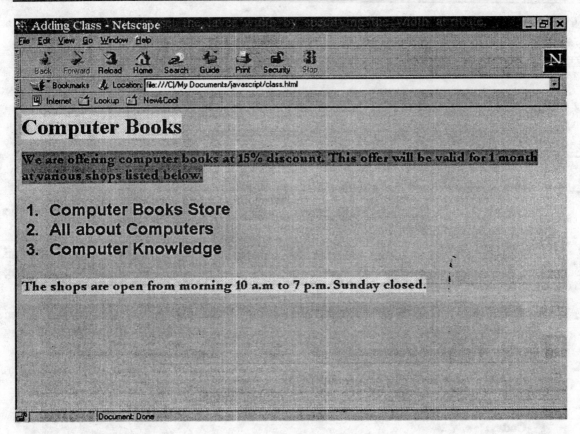

Working with Layers

The different layer properties are as follows:

Position. You can set the layer position into three formats.

　　Static. Position when defines as static cannot be moved. Generally this is a default format.

　　Absolute. Position when defines as absolute appears according to the co-ordinate given.

　　Relative. Position when defines as relative have an offset from the static position where the element have been laid.

Left – You can set the left position of the layer, which is in relative to the browser window.

Top – You can set the top position of the layer, which is in relative to the browser window.

Height – You can set the layer height by specifying the height attribute.

Width – You can set the layer width by specifying the width attribute.

Background-color – You can set the background-color of the layer by specifying a color.

Layer-background-color – Specifies a background color for a whole layer.

Background-image – You can set an image background in a layer using background-image.

Layer-Background-image – Specifies a background image for a whole layer.

Color – You can set the text color of the layer using the color attribute.

Clip – This is used for clipping a rectangle for an item.

Overflow – This includes three values none, clip and scroll. It indicates whether the clipping rectangle clips an item or to view the whole item using scrollbar.

Z-index – You can set an index of the items using z-index. Starting from 1 you can set the increasing number to add layer of the top of one layer. This gives an overlapping effect.

Visibility – This property makes an item visible. It includes three values visible, hidden and inherit. Visible makes an item visible, hidden hides it and inherit - inherits the visibility of another item where it appears.

For ex. Viewing an item in a paragraph.

Follow the code, which displays functionality of layers

Code :

```
<Html>
<Head>
<Title>Layer</Title>
</Head>
<Body>
<Center><H1>Music Program</H1></Center>
<div id="layer1";
style="position:static; font-size:20; color:blue">
<P>We are going to organize a Music Program at Netaji Indoor Stadium on 25<Sup>th
</Sup>December.
So join us and enjoy the Christmas Night.</P>
</div>
<div id="layer2"
style="position:static; font-size:18; background-color:pink; color:blue">
<Center><P>The program is organized by Young Bengal Students Group.</P></Center>
</div>
```

```
<div id="layer3"
style="position:static; Left:50; Top:200; Width:300; Height:100; Font-style:Italic;
Font-weight:bold; Font-size=16; background-color:yellow; color:red">
<Ul>
<Li>Holy Band Group
<Li>Chindren's Band Group
<Li>Teen's Band Group
</Ul>
</div>
<div id="layer4"
style="position:absolute; Left:400; Top:250; Height:100; Font-weight:bold; font-size=14;
background-color:red; color:white">
<P>The Names of the Participants</P>
<OL>
<Li>Rahul
<Li>Minu
<Li>Tina
<Li>Mohan
</OL>
</div>
<div id="layer5"
style="position:absolute; Left:100; Height:100; Width:200; Top:300; Font-weight:bold;
Font-size=18; background-color:orange; color:blue">
Tickets available at Counter of Rs.200(Front Seat), Rs.150(Chair), Rs.100(Gallery).
</div>
<div id="layer6"
style="position:absolute; Left:400; Height:70; Width:150; Top:400; Font-size:20;
background-color:blue; color:white">
So Hurry Up!
</div>
</Body>
</Html>
```

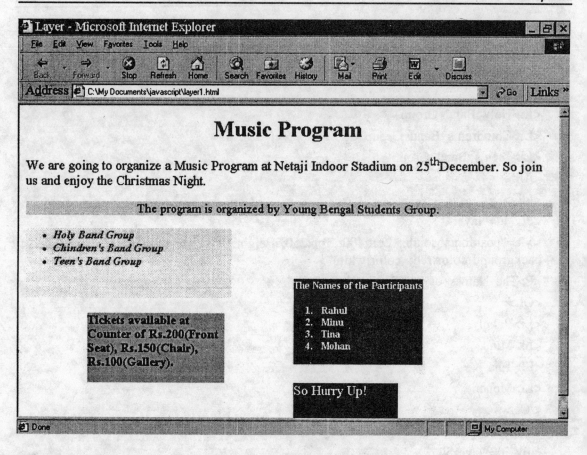

Working with Show and Hide property of the DIV tag

This example shows the Show and Hide property of the DIV tag. The image hides when the mouse pointer is placed on it.

Code :

```
<Html>
<Head>
<Title>ShowHide</Title></Head>
<Body>
<Script Language="JavaScript">
function image1_onmouseover()
{
    image1.style.visibility="visible";
    image2.style.visibility="hidden";
}
```

```
function img_onmouseout()
{
    image1.style.visibility="hidden";
    image2.style.visibility="visible";
}
function image2_onmouseover()
{
    image1.style.visibility="hidden";
    image2.style.visibility="visible";
}
</Script>
```

<H2><U>Working with Show and Hide property by using the DIV tag.</U></H2>

```
<center>
<DIV style="visibility : visible "onmouseover=" image1_onmouseover();"
onmouseout="img_onmouseout();">
<Img id=image1 src="C:\My Documents\webdesign\gift8.jpg" height="150"
width="150">
</center>
</DIV>
<center>
<DIV style="visibility: visible" onmouseover="image2_onmouseover();"
onmouseout="img_onmouseout();">
<Img id=image2 src="C:\My Documents\webdesign\gift6.jpg" height="150"
width="150">
</center>
</DIV>
</Body>
</Html>
```

image1 is visible and image2 is invisible

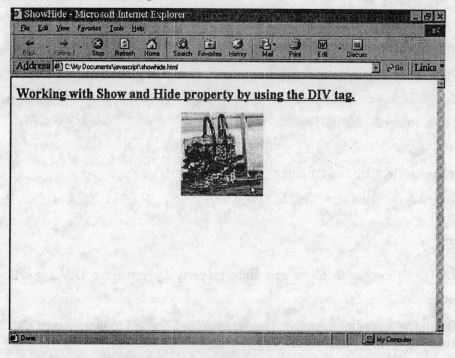

image2 is visible and image1 is invisible

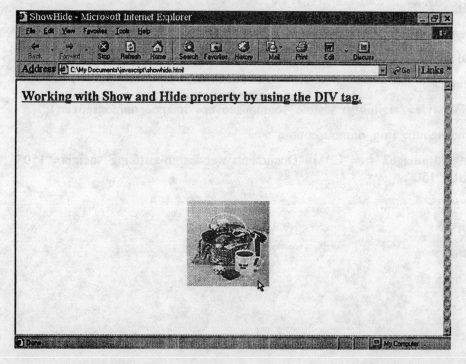

PLANNING

How to plan while creating web pages?

One thing is to be very clear while creating a web page. You should plan for it because sometime it happens that – to show their talent they jumbled the page with unnecessary things. Till now you have studied HTML, DHTML and Java Script. You have created web pages using the different tags discussed above but when you are going to create commercial web page you need proper planning. So follow the steps to create a web page.

1. Write down the purpose of creating the web page. Then write the required contents. Note the type of image you want to add and find out whether it is available in your PC or not. If not collect it from elsewhere like – Internet or from any picture CDs.

2. After setting the plan create the HTML file. Add all the features like text, headings, images, frames etc. as per your requirement. Write the code in a text editor like notepad and save it with a HTML extension.

3. Then add the script tags and style sheet information. In this part you need to add style sheet features like heading colors, font attributes, classes etc. and script tags, which includes scrolling message, functions, displaying message etc.

4. Then make the page dynamic by adding interactive features. This is the last step where you need to add necessary animations and different features, which makes the web attractive.

These steps will certainly help you to create meani. g full, attractive web pages.